Tax Guide 205

SMALL
C & S
CORPORATIONS

by

Holmes F. Crouch
Tax Specialist

Published by

Allyear Tax Guides

20484 Glen Brae Drive
Saratoga, CA 95070

ISBN 0-944817-60-2

LCCN 00-132600

Printed in U.S.A.

Series 200
Investors & Businesses

Tax Guide 205

SMALL C & S CORPORATIONS

For other titles in print, see page 224.

The author: **Holmes F. Crouch**
For more about the author, see page 221.

PREFACE

If you are a knowledge-seeking **taxpayer** looking for information, this book can be helpful to you. It is designed to be read — from cover to cover — in about eight hours. Or, it can be "skim-read" in about 30 minutes.

Either way, you are treated to **tax knowledge** . . . *beyond the ordinary*. The "beyond" is that which cannot be found in IRS publications, FedWorld on-line services, tax software programs, Internet chatrooms, or e-mail bulletins.

Taxpayers have different levels of interest in a selected subject. For this reason, this book starts with introductory fundamentals and progresses onward. You can verify the progression by chapter and section in the table of contents. In the text, "applicable law" is quoted in pertinent part. Key phrases and key tax forms are emphasized. Real-life examples are given . . . in down-to-earth style.

This book has 12 chapters. This number provides depth without cross-subject rambling. Each chapter starts with a head summary of meaningful information.

To aid in your skim-reading, informative diagrams and tables are placed strategically throughout the text. By leafing through page by page, reading the summaries and section headings, and glancing at the diagrams and tables, you can get a good handle on the matters covered.

Effort has been made to update and incorporate all of the latest tax law changes that are *significant* to the title subject. However, "beyond the ordinary" does not encompass every conceivable variant of fact and law that might give rise to protracted dispute and litigation. Consequently, if a particular statement or paragraph is crucial to your own specific case, you are urged to seek professional counseling. Otherwise, the information presented is general and is designed for a broad range of reader interests.

The Author

INTRODUCTION

A C corporation is defined in the Internal Revenue Code as an incorporated entity which is not an S corporation [Sec. 1361(a)(2)]. An S corporation is defined as—

A domestic small business corporation . . . which does not have more than 75 shareholders, and . . . [which has only] *one class of stock* [Sec. 1361(b)(1)].

The practical effect of these definitions is that a C corporation is regarded as a "regular" (trade or business) corporation, unlimited in size, whereas an S corporation is viewed exclusively as a "small business" entity. However, there is no prohibition against a C corporation also being a small business entity.

How small does a C corporation have to be, to be tax considered "small"?

To answer this question, we rely on IRC Section 448: *Limitation on Use of Cash Method of Accounting.* For C corporations, the cash method is allowed only for those entities whose *gross receipts,* when averaged over a 3-taxable-year period *. . . do not exceed $5,000,000* [Sec. 448(c)(1)]. Thus, for our purposes, a small C or S corporation is one whose gross receipts for the latest taxable year do not exceed $5,000,000 (5 million).

The $5,000,000 figure is also a threshold beyond which the issuance of private stock is prohibited by the Securities and Exchange Commission (SEC). Under Rule 505 of SEC Regulation D, offers and sales of securities up to $5,000,000 (to no more than 35 purchasers) are exempt from public registration. However, offerings above $1,000,000 must be *disclosed* to the SEC. This is done in a disclosure statement which identifies those investors who are "accredited" (having a net worth over $1,000,000) and those who are nonaccredited.

In certain sections of the Tax Code (e.g. Secs. 465, 469, 542), the concept of a *closely-held corporation* is raised. A closely-held entity is a C corporation in which five or fewer individuals own (directly or indirectly) more than 50 percent of the voting stock of the corporation. Hence, the term "closely held" implies "small," whether it be a C or S entity. The term also implies strictly **privately issued** stock . . . between family, friends, and close business associates.

The long and short of the above is that virtually every small C or S corporation is TAX SUSPECT. From an IRS perspective, closely held corporations — also called: "close corporations" — are used as tax shelters and tax avoidance devices by the controlling owners. To said persons, the corporate entity is a lucrative source for enhancing the salaries of officers and managers when business is good, for writing off most of their personal expenditures for travel, entertainment, fancy cars and boats, and furniture and fixtures for the home, and for placing family members on the payroll who contribute little or nothing to the business enterprise.

When business is bad, the controlling owners "borrow" from the corporation with no-interest loans. Rarely are such loans ever paid back. Venders and suppliers (who are priority accounts payable) are kept in a holding pattern while the owners deplete the assets by paying themselves instead of paying off corporate debts . . . including taxes. Then, as a last resort, the corporate shield is used to fend off ownership liability should the business fail, be sued, or go bankrupt.

If the business flourishes, and the combination of receipts and assets approaches the $10,000,000 mark, there are visions of merging with an existing public corporation or "going public" on one's own. We encourage these visions, and will discuss them in Chapter 12 hereof.

Meanwhile, our premise is that a small C or S corporation can play a vital role in the enhancement of personal wealth by those owners who are prudent and visionary. That is, IF . . . such owners will do things tax right. Doing things tax right means operating the business as an entity separate and apart from one's personal ego. If you can — and will — do this, you can emerge from an IRS audit with a "no change." This could be one of your proudest moments. Helping you achieve other proud moments in your corporate affairs is what this book is all about.

CONTENTS

Chapter   **Page**

1. CORPORATION BONA FIDES............ **1-1**

    The Liability Limitation Issue............................. 1- 2
    Articles of Incorporation..................................... 1- 3
    Why Incorporate in Delaware?......................... 1- 6
    Adoption of Bylaws 1- 7
    Shares & Share Certificates............................. 1- 8
    Shareholder Meetings & Minutes.................... 1-12
    What Constitutes "True" Minutes.................... 1-13
    Dilemma When No Minutes 1-14
    Inquiries the IRS Makes.................................... 1-17

2. ELECTION OF S STATUS..................... **2-1**

    Subchapter S Overview..................................... 2- 2
    How S Status Defined.. 2- 4
    Counting the Shareholders................................ 2- 6
    Unanimous Consent Required........................... 2- 8
    Timing of the Election 2- 9
    Elect on Form 2553.. 2-10
    Revocation by Majority Vote............................. 2-13
    Reinstatement after Termination...................... 2-15

3. FORMS 1120 AND 1120S **3-1**

    Introductory Differences.................................... 3- 2
    Income & Deduction Blocks.............................. 3- 4
    Pages 2 and 3 Compared................................... 3- 5
    Capital Gains & Losses...................................... 3- 9
    How Tax Items Compare.................................... 3-11
    How Tax Rates Compare 3-12
    Schedule K-1 (Form 1120S)............................... 3-14
    Schedule L: Balance Sheets 3-18

Chapter   **Page**

4. COMPENSATION OF OFFICERS **4-1**

Business Necessity Essential 4- 2
Active Business Requirement 4- 5
What is a "Reasonable" Salary? 4- 6
General Factors for Decisions 4- 8
Special Factors for Scrutiny 4-10
The "Dexsil" Appeals Case 4-12
The "Leonard Pipeline" Case 4-14
Treatment of Excess Compensation 4-16

5. WHEN UNDERCAPITALIZED **5-1**

What is Expected of You 5- 2
Stockholder Reluctance 5- 4
Below-Market Loans 5- 5
Section 1244 Stock 5- 8
Conditions for 1244 Stock 5- 9
Payroll Withholdings & Taxes 5-13
The 100% Trust Fund Penalty 5-14
Responsible Person Defined 5-16
Scrutiny of Employee Benefits 5-18
Immediate Assessment Authority 5-19

6. METHODS OF ACCOUNTING **6-1**

Selection of Tax Year 6- 2
Change of Tax Year 6- 4
Dominance of Section 446 .... 6- 5
Must Clearly Reflect Income 6- 7
Cash vs. Accrual Methods 6- 9
Inventory Capitalization 6-10
Valuing Ending Inventory 6-12

Chapter	Page

7. BALANCE SHEET BALANCING 7-1

Clarification of Bad Debts	7- 2
Asset Listing Review................................	7- 3
Now, the Liabilities Side...........................	7- 6
Stockholders' Equity.................................	7- 7
Accumulated Earnings	7- 9
Treasury Stock Explained.........................	7-11
Schedule M-1: Reconciliations	7-13
Schedule M-2: C Corporations.................	7-15
Schedule M-2: S Corporations	7-17

8. CAUTIONS RE PHC STATUS 8-1

S Corporations Unaffected	8- 2
Avoid Confusion with PSC.......................	8- 3
Overview of PHC Statutes	8- 5
PHC Income Defined................................	8- 6
Adjusted Ordinary Gross Income	8- 7
The 60% PHC Income "Test"	8- 9
The 50% Ownership Test...........................	8-11
Constructive Ownership of Stock.............	8-12
Overview of Schedule PH........................	8-13
Computing Undistributed PHC Income..............	8-16
Cheaper to Distribute	8-17

9. FOREIGN ACTIVITY QUESTIONS..... 9-1

The Most Common Question......................	9- 2
Form TD F 90-22.1..................................	9- 4
The Next Common Question	9- 7
Commentary on Foreign Trusts	9- 8
C Corporations: Question A....................	9-11
If "Yes" to Question A: Form 5471	9-13
C Corporations: Question B	9-14
Concluding Commentary	9-16

Chapter		Page

10. ITEMS NOT DEDUCTIBLE **10-1**

Starting at the Top 10- 2
When Business Purpose Not Shown 10- 3
Life Insurance Premiums 10- 5
Using the Corporation as Intermediary 10- 7
Company Sponsored Entertainment, Etc. 10- 8
Example: Clear Business Purpose 10-11
Executive Travel Expenses 10-12
Luxury Autos, Boats, Planes 10-15
Personal Use Affidavits 10-17

11. BASIS IN STOCK HELD **11-1**

Shareholders Ledger Not Relevant 11- 2
Contributions to Capital 11- 3
When Services Exchanged 11- 6
Founder Shares: Basis In 11- 8
Additional Stock for Cash 11-10
Taxable Stock Dividends 11-11
Nontaxable Distributions Reduce Basis 11-13
Basis in Gifted Stock 11-15
Basis in Inherited Stock 11-17

12. SELL, MERGE, OR GO PUBLIC **12-1**

Preliminary Decisions to Make 12- 2
Instructions to Committee 12- 4
Effect of Sale on Shareholders 12- 5
Effect of Sale on Corporation 12- 7
Treatment as "Sale of Assets" 12- 9
Stock-for-Stock Exchanges 12-11
Types of Reorganizations 12-12
The Merger Process Exemplified 12-14
Precautions When "Going Public" 12-16
Tax Law Statement 12-18
Issuance Goal: 10 Times Assets 12-19

1

CORPORATION BONA FIDES

> The First Indicator Of NONSERIOUS Corporate Intentions Is Any Failure To Amend And Change The Initial "Articles And Bylaws" Boilerplated By The Incorporators. A Second Indicator Is The Absence Of Share Certificates And A "Shareholders Ledger." A Third Indicator Is Inattention To Annual And Special Meetings Of DIRECTORS And SHARE-HOLDERS, And Disregard For An Authenticated "Minutes Book." A Fourth Indicator Is Failure To Declare Dividends In a Profit-Making Year. A Fifth Indicator Is Raising The Compensation Of Officers In A Loss Year, Without Any Change In The Bylaws Justifying The Raise.

What makes a corporation so different from that of a human being? Why is the difference important when conducting business in closely-held form? After all, business is business, and people conduct business in whatever manner that works. Why should the IRS or anyone else object to this?

First off, a corporation is a legal entity created and franchised under State law. It is a creature of law: not of man. Its incubation period may vary from several weeks to several years. After application and the payment of a fee, "birth" is indicated by a Certificate of Incorporation. The certificate is numbered and authenticated by the Secretary of State for the domicile where the corporation is home based. Once so certified, the entity has indefinite life. It does not fade away or die of natural causes. It has to be formally dissolved, which again requires certification by the Secretary of State.

Once formulated, the corporation can be "sliced up" into small parts called: *shares*. The shares can be sold or exchanged legally, though care is required not to sell private shares publicly.

Consequently, in this introductory chapter, we want to describe the particular features of a corporation that make it stand out from the personas of the principal shareholders thereof. In other words, to an outside disinterested party, is the entity really a corporation in fact? Or is it an alter ego used a shield and sham to avoid liability to customers and creditors . . . and to the IRS? Is it being run as a tax shelter, or is it being run with a business purpose that will stand the test of time? To the public at large, a business conducted in corporate form — if truly bona fide — exudes prestige and status and the expectation of continuity of life. The expectation of its declaring bankruptcy is taboo.

The Liability Limitation Issue

For years past, small business entities have sought corporation status as a means for limiting liability in the event of misfortune. The belief was that, in the event of a creditor claim or customer lawsuit, liability would be limited to the net worth (assets minus liabilities) of the corporate entity. This concept has stood the business community reasonably well for large and superlarge corporations of the day. But, for small, medium, and closely held entities, the corporate shield is easily pierced with (often wild) allegations of fraud and misrepresentation. This "piercing" exposes the controlling shareholders to personal liability for their corporate acts. As a result, many honorable business owners have had their personal lives financially destroyed.

Within recent years, the explosion of lawsuits against corporations has caused many small businesses to seek noncorporate entity form, with narrowly limited legal liability. This struggle has been the genesis of the LLC concept: Limited Liability Company. The first state statute granting limited liability to noncorporate entities occurred in 1977. The State of Wyoming was the first in the nation to do so. Today, all 50 states, along with the District of Columbia, have LLC statutes.

What is the essence key of an LLC statute?

It is that no LLC member is personally responsible for LLC liability in excess of his contribution of capital or property to the entity enterprise. This is the guarantee of state law. The net effect is that any liability established in excess of the pooled capital of the LLC members is treated as a *nonrecourse* item. That is, the excess liability is not recoverable.

Unfortunately, LLC statutes tend to cause small business entities to be thinly capitalized. The term "thin capitalization" generally implies an equity-to-debt ratio of 0.25 or less. In other words, with an equity ratio of 0.25, the operating debt is three times $(1.00 - 0.25 = 0.75)$ the operating capital available for liability recourse purposes. Under these circumstances, customers, creditors, and even the IRS get queasy when the equity ratio drops below 0.50.

For federal tax purposes, an LLC is treated as a *general partnership*: not as a corporation. This is because in such a partnership all members are jointly and severally liable for the tax consequences of the entity endeavor. You cannot use state law to limit your federal tax liabilities (period)!

With the above in mind, we drop the subject of LLCs entirely. We brought the subject up only to stress the importance of the liability issue, and to point out that one of the elements of a bona fide small corporation is having an equity ratio of 0.50 or higher. If this ratio is operationally unreasonable, then having adequate liability insurance becomes a "must."

Articles of Incorporation

An eligible entity for incorporation is a trade or business carried on for profit, in which participants share in the profits therefrom. Although this concept of an entity applies to all forms of private enterprise, the central tax determinator is *material participation* in an active, ongoing, nonpassive endeavor. The goal of the endeavor, to one extent or another, is to design, manufacture, or sell a product or service to the public at large. This precludes — certainly for closely held entities — banking, insurance, lending, investing, and gratuitous-type activities. Accordingly, a first step in becoming a small business corporation is to prepare and submit (to state authorities) your Articles of Incorporation.

Each state has its own Corporations Code. In such code, there are legal procedures for forming a corporation under that state's law. Usually, these procedures are found in a dominant chapter titled: General Corporation Law. Within this chapter, there is usually a section titled: *Articles of Incorporation; Required Provisions* . . . or words to this effect. Typically, the articles of incorporation shall set forth:

(a) The name of the corporation.

(b) The purpose of the corporation . . . *to engage in any lawful act or activity for which a corporation may be organized under the General Corporation Law of the State of* _____ .

(c) The name and address *in this state* of the corporation's initial agent for service of process.

(d) The total number of shares which the corporation is authorized to issue (if only one class of shares).

(e) If more than one class or series, the total number of authorized shares of each class or series, together with . . . *the rights, preferences, privileges, and restrictions granted or imposed upon the respective classes or series.*

Except for multiple classes and series of shares, item (e) above, no formal legalisms are required. A one-page document will suffice. Contact the Secretary of State in your state capital and request forms, samples, and instructions. You do not need any prestigious legal firm to do such simple tasks. Follow the general procedures that we outline in Figure 1.1. With the samples provided by the Secretary of State's office, prepare your own articles and submit them as instructed. Or, you may engage a professional incorporator to do the initial paperwork.

There will be a filing fee which will be invoiced to the "initial incorporator(s)" by the Secretary of State. After the fee is received (order of $100 or so), a **Certificate of Incorporation** will be issued. This will be an impressive multi-colored document with the state seal gold-embossed thereon. There will also be a *corporation*

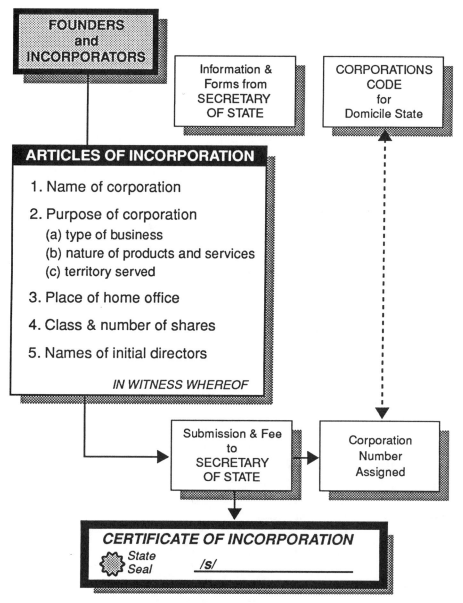

Fig. 1.1 - Basic Requirements for Obtaining "Certificate of Incorporation"

number assigned. This number is simply a filing indexation for public records maintained by the Secretary of State, Division of Corporations.

Why Incorporate in Delaware?

It takes only one person to actually form a corporation. Furthermore, that person — called "the incorporator" — does not have to be a participant in corporate operations, once the Secretary of State has issued a Certificate of Incorporation. It is for this reason that temporary agents (attorneys, paralegals, CPAs) can be engaged to achieve certification. Once this is done, the "powers and duties" of the incorporator terminate. Thereupon the founding directors of the corporation take over. This practice has led to many Delaware corporations being formed throughout the U.S.

The State of Delaware (the second smallest in the nation) is dubbed the "corporation state." It is alleged that more than half of the *Fortune 500* megacorporations have been incorporated there (at one time or another). This legendary status has prompted many paralegals residing in Delaware to tout nationwide the availability of their services. For a fee of about $500 or so, a Delaware incorporator will "do all of the paperwork."

How much paperwork really is involved?

Answer: For a closely held corporation it is **one preprinted page**. That's it! All of the necessary legal clauses are already printed on the one-page form. There are five blank lines for entering: (1) name of corporation, (2) name and address of registered agent in Delaware, (3) number of shares and par value, (4) name and address of initial directors and stockholder(s), and (5) certifying signature, date, and place.

Additionally, the incorporation fee includes a 2-inch thick looseleaf binder with your corporation name bold-printed conspicuously thereon. The binder consists of boilerplate stock certificate forms, model bylaws, sample minutes of meetings, and instructions on the appointment of directors and officers. It also contains numerous lined blank pages headed: *Notes*. The purpose of the binder is to provide you with all the paperwork *forms* for setting up business in Delaware. Other than filling in the five blank lines on the Certificate of Incorporation, the intended corporate officers (President and Secretary) have to do **all** of the follow-through paperwork.

Why would persons in the states of Alaska, Texas, and California, for example, with a combined land mass over 1,000,000 square miles) want to incorporate in the tiny State of Delaware (with a land mass of 2,000$^+$ square miles)? Is it because Delaware was the first state to join the Union in 1787 with the motto: "Liberty and Independence"? Even if so, wouldn't this raise questions in customer, creditor, and employee minds about the true intentions of corporate activities?

The truth is: There is no logical reason to incorporate in Delaware, when doing business and establishing a home base in, for example, California. The incorporation procedures in California are just about as liberal as those in Delaware. Furthermore, the out-of-state incorporation provides little or no legal protection, no stock issuance benefits, and absolutely no tax protection whatsoever. It shows much better good faith to incorporate in the state where you expect to initially do business.

Adoption of Bylaws

Once a Certificate of Incorporation is at hand, the first order of business is to elect/appoint a Board of Directors. For a closely held corporation, this is usually a self-election, self-appointment process to get things going. No formal elections or meetings take place. It is by mutual consent that Persons A, B, and C will become Directors A, B, and C, respectively. They can agree among themselves that each director owns a specified number of shares, proportionate to his/her relative (expected) contribution of capital to the forming corporation. This share agreement should be written down, with each director signing and dating it.

The bylaws of a corporation represent a contractual obligation between the directors and the state law of the state of incorporation. The bylaws are also a contract between the directors and elected/appointed officers/managers of the business. The bylaws set down the terms and conditions, powers and duties, and responsibilities and obligations of the parties thereto. The bylaws can expand on the purpose, nature, and scope of the business, the territory of operations, and the accountability for official acts by the managers thereof. Once adopted, the bylaws must be made available for inspection by all subsequent shareholders in the enterprise.

The function and general contents of corporate bylaws are depicted in Figure 1.2. Specific contents are designated in the Corporations Code of the state of incorporation. The indicated contents are "all over the place" for small, medium, large, and superlarge corporate entities. A better way is to search among your small-corporation colleagues (by phone, fax, e-mail, or Internet) for permission to borrow and use as a model that entity's existing set of bylaws. Edit and reword them to conform to your own situation. Then engage a local attorney skilled in corporation law, to help finalize the (initial) bylaws for you.

Once prepared and adopted, most bylaws are set aside and forgotten. It is only when a lawsuit is filed (by a customer, supplier, creditor, shareholder, employee, or some injured party) that the bylaws are brought to life. Thus, the idea is to prepare the bylaws for the day **when** — NOT "if" — the lawsuit comes. The seriousness with which the bylaws are prepared and *followed* is a good indicator of the bona fideness of the corporate business.

When the bylaws are formulated, an initial directors' meeting "shall be called." The bylaws "shall be adopted" by a majority vote. Minutes of the meeting "shall be made." Included in the minutes are instructions on how the bylaws are to be amended, as the business develops and unfolds. A *Minutes Book* "shall be maintained." Keeping an updated minutes book is another indicator of a bona fide corporation.

Shares & Share Certificates

Small and closely held corporations tend to be sloppy about shareholder recordkeeping chores. Much of the required information on the issuance of shares is kept in the heads of the principal owners. Rarely are actual share certificates issued. Although electronic files may be used to track the issuance, contributions of capital, redemptions, transfers, and other matters, the actual issuance of authenticated paper certificates is highly

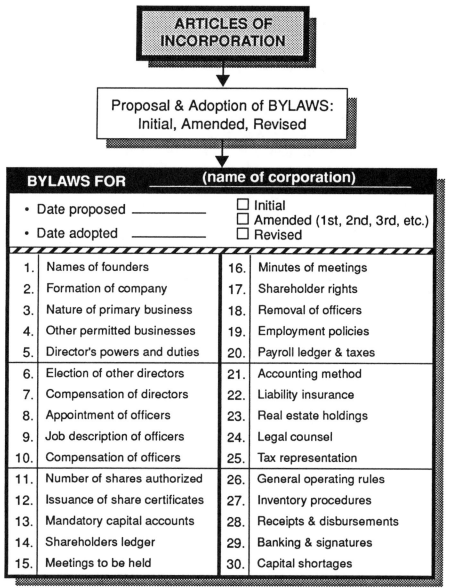

ARTICLES OF INCORPORATION

↓

Proposal & Adoption of BYLAWS:
Initial, Amended, Revised

↓

BYLAWS FOR _____ **(name of corporation)**

- Date proposed _____   ☐ Initial
                            ☐ Amended (1st, 2nd, 3rd, etc.)
- Date adopted _____   ☐ Revised

No.		No.	
1.	Names of founders	16.	Minutes of meetings
2.	Formation of company	17.	Shareholder rights
3.	Nature of primary business	18.	Removal of officers
4.	Other permitted businesses	19.	Employment policies
5.	Director's powers and duties	20.	Payroll ledger & taxes
6.	Election of other directors	21.	Accounting method
7.	Compensation of directors	22.	Liability insurance
8.	Appointment of officers	23.	Real estate holdings
9.	Job description of officers	24.	Legal counsel
10.	Compensation of officers	25.	Tax representation
11.	Number of shares authorized	26.	General operating rules
12.	Issuance of share certificates	27.	Inventory procedures
13.	Mandatory capital accounts	28.	Receipts & disbursements
14.	Shareholders ledger	29.	Banking & signatures
15.	Meetings to be held	30.	Capital shortages

Fig. 1.2 - Items for Inclusion in Corporate "Bylaws"

recommended. Not only does this help to persuade investors of the above-board intentions of the corporation, it also persuades the IRS, state taxing agencies, and the legal profession that you have the necessary records on each shareholder. You can design your own certificates, or you can purchase predesigned certificates with adequate blank lines and preprinted (legal) wording to meet your needs.

Check your state's Corporations Code for the chapter on: *Shares and Share Certificates.* There are certain procedures to follow, such as a resolution by the board of directors setting forth the total numbers of shares to be issued; establishing the rights, preferences, privileges, and restrictions on the shares issued; requiring that records be kept; and designating which officer of the corporation (by title) shall authenticate each share certificate that is issued, transferred, or redeemed. Procedures for the replacement of lost, stolen, or destroyed shares should be established. The board also should designate which officer of the corporation shall be responsible for maintaining a *Shareholders Ledger* at all times. The general contents of such a ledger are summarized in Figure 1.3.

To give you a taste of what the California Corporations Code says about the issuance of shares, we cite three (short) extractions therefrom:

CCC Sec. 410(a) — *Every subscriber to shares and every person to whom shares are originally issued is **liable to the corporation** for the full consideration agreed to be paid for the shares.* [Emphasis added.]

CCC Sec. 416(a) — *Every holder of shares in a corporation **shall be entitled** to have a certificate signed in the name of the corporation by the* [authenticating officer], *certifying the number of shares . . . owned by the shareholder.* [Emphasis added.]

CCC Sec. 418(a)-(d) — *There shall also appear on the certificate, the initial transaction statement, and written statements that the shares are **subject to restrictions**, . . . subject to being assessed* [to meet designated liabilities], *. . . being a closely held corporation the **maximum number of holders of shares** cannot exceed_____, . . . and any attempted voluntary inter vivos transfer of shares that exceed the* *maximum number of holders indicated . . . **shall be void.*** [Emphasis added.]

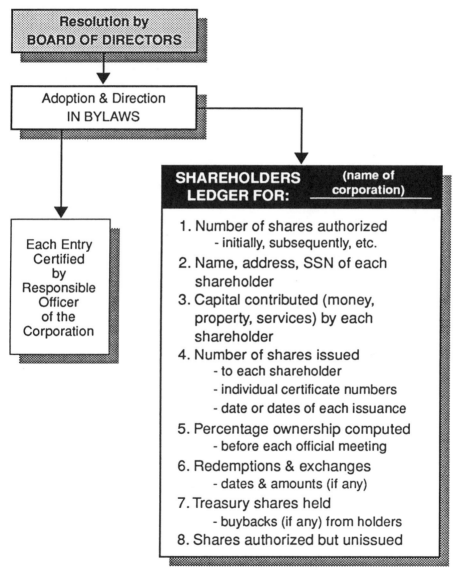

Resolution by BOARD OF DIRECTORS

Adoption & Direction IN BYLAWS

Each Entry Certified by Responsible Officer of the Corporation

SHAREHOLDERS LEDGER FOR: (name of corporation)

1. Number of shares authorized
   - initially, subsequently, etc.
2. Name, address, SSN of each shareholder
3. Capital contributed (money, property, services) by each shareholder
4. Number of shares issued
   - to each shareholder
   - individual certificate numbers
   - date or dates of each issuance
5. Percentage ownership computed
   - before each official meeting
6. Redemptions & exchanges
   - dates & amounts (if any)
7. Treasury shares held
   - buybacks (if any) from holders
8. Shares authorized but unissued

Fig. 1.3 - General Contents of a "Shareholders Ledger"

You should conclude from the above that the issuance of shares in a corporation is serious business. This is so, no matter how small the capitalization, or how few shareholders there may be.

Nothing exposes the disingenousness of corporate intentions more than when a principal owner pledges $100,000 to the capital formation, but only puts up $10,000. He treats the $90,000 shortage as a "loan" from the corporation. He promises to pay the $90,000 back out of his proportionate share (based on his $100,000 pledge) of the earnings and profits of the enterprise. In other words, he is relying on the gullibility of other shareholders to let the corporation use their capital to make $90,000 on a pledge for which only $10,000 is at risk. This is no way to run a corporation; it is the way to run a sham.

Now you know why it is so important to have a **Shareholders Ledger** maintained and updated at all times. When a share issuance and subscription date is set by the board of directors, any shortage in full consideration pledge must result in a corresponding reduction in voting shares issued to that pledger. Wheelers and dealers should be put on notice at the outset that they are expected to contribute full-risk capital. Otherwise, do not incorporate.

Shareholder Meetings & Minutes

In addition to shenanigans on capital pledges, close corporations have another glaring fault. They rarely hold annual shareholder meetings. If, occasionally, such a meeting is held, minutes are rarely ever kept. The mindset seems to be that, even though state law requires such meetings (and the keeping of minutes) no less frequently than once annually, it is only necessary for large corporations to do so. Shareholder meetings are not a voluntary matter; they are a legal requirement.

Again, using the California Corporations Code as an example, we cite the following relevant items:

CCC Sec. 600(b) — *An annual meeting of shareholders **shall be held** for the election of directors on a date, at a time, and at a place stated . . . in the bylaws. . . . Any other proper business may be transacted at the annual meeting.* [Emphasis added.]

CCC Sec. 600(c) — *If there is a failure to hold the annual meeting . . . for a period of 15 months after the organization of the corporation or after its last annual meeting, the Superior Court of the proper county **may summarily order** a meeting to be held, upon the application of any shareholder. . . .* [Emphasis added.]

CCC Sec. 700(a) — *Except as may be otherwise provided in the articles* [of incorporation], *each outstanding share, regardless of class, shall be entitled to one vote on each matter submitted to a vote of shareholders.*

What usually happens in a close corporation is this. The founder and patriarch, or whoever has the greatest single number of shares, conducts all required meetings on the fly. He does so by phone, fax, e-mail, and momentary personal contact, during a coffee break or another chance meeting. He states that no new matters have come up to require any regular, special, or joint meeting (of shareholders and directors). He accepts any acknowledgment as implied consent to waive the meeting. The corporate secretary is then instructed to prepare a perfunctory set of minutes authenticating that the meeting (designated in the articles and bylaws) is officially waived. Thereafter, business is conducted in a cavalier manner, the founder/patriarch knowing full well that he has the controlling votes to do so. Invariably, the business takes on the persona and alter ego of he/she/they who hold the majority of shares.

What Constitutes "True" Minutes

Every corporation must have a set of articles and, separately, a set of bylaws. Professional incorporators are well aware of this basic requirement. It is for this reason that the initial set of articles and bylaws is boilerplated to pass muster in the state of incorporation. These preprinted articles and bylaws are *not* frozen in concrete. They are expected to be changed as the founding directors take over and as operational practices unfold.

Amending the articles and bylaws, or changing them altogether, and resolving corporate policy matters are what the purposes of official corporate meetings are all about. There are four types of such meetings, namely: (1) directors' meetings, (2) shareholders' meetings, (3) joint meetings (directors and shareholders), and (4) special meetings (may be joint or not). Every meeting is to be preceded with a written notification to eligible attendees stating the time, date, place, and items for discussion. Once a meeting is held and adjourned, official minutes shall be prepared. No particular formality is required, so long as each set of minutes is sequentially titled. For example—

- Founders' Initial Meeting
- Directors' First Annual Meeting
- Shareholders' Third Annual Meeting
- First Joint Meeting of Directors and Shareholders
- Third Special Meeting of Shareholders

The minutes of every meeting shall be duly authenticated *under penalties of perjury* that the statements recorded are *true, correct, and complete.* The jurat clause (as it is called) is signed by two corporate officers, usually the President and the Secretary.

When the minutes are authenticated, each set should be filed in the corporation's *Minutes Book.* This book may be a separate file of its own, or it may be included in other corporate files that constitute the *Corporation Manual* of the entity undertaking.

We present in Figure 1.4 an outline of what the Minutes Book should contain. We also indicate the general contents of what the record of a meeting should show. We also urge that you make inquiries to your colleagues in comparable-size corporations as to the regularity and format of their minutes-keeping procedures. Particularly search out those closely held corporations which have recently experienced court litigation and/or an IRS audit. Absorbing their experiences will convince you, we think, of the importance of a true Minutes Book.

Dilemma When No Minutes

For a closely held corporation, we realize that calling periodic director/shareholder meetings is a painful chore. All the directors

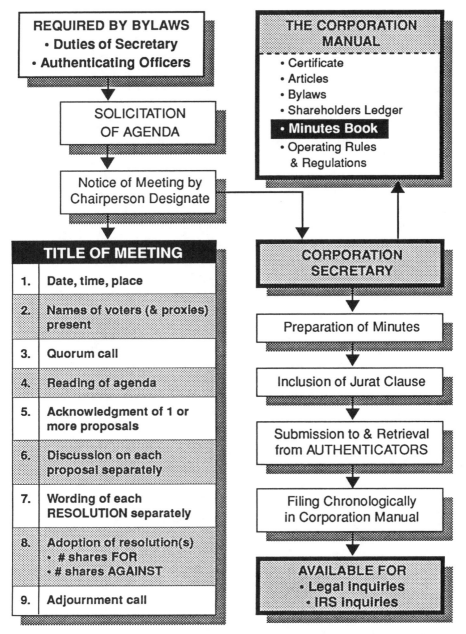

REQUIRED BY BYLAWS
- **Duties of Secretary**
- **Authenticating Officers**

SOLICITATION
OF AGENDA

Notice of Meeting by
Chairperson Designate

THE CORPORATION MANUAL
- Certificate
- Articles
- Bylaws
- Shareholders Ledger
- **Minutes Book**
- Operating Rules
  & Regulations

	TITLE OF MEETING
1.	Date, time, place
2.	Names of voters (& proxies) present
3.	Quorum call
4.	Reading of agenda
5.	Acknowledgment of 1 or more proposals
6.	Discussion on each proposal separately
7.	Wording of each RESOLUTION separately
8.	Adoption of resolution(s) • # shares FOR • # shares AGAINST
9.	Adjournment call

CORPORATION SECRETARY

Preparation of Minutes

Inclusion of Jurat Clause

Submission to & Retrieval
from AUTHENTICATORS

Filing Chronologically
in Corporation Manual

AVAILABLE FOR
- **Legal inquiries**
- **IRS inquiries**

Fig. 1.4 - Role and Contents of Corporate "Minutes Book"

and shareholders know each other. They converse and gather consensus from time to time on an "as needed" basis. Formal minutes of meetings are seldom kept because "everyone knows the situation." Is that so? Here's a true life/death example where no outside litigation occurred, and the corporation was not under IRS audit.

After a husband and wife with two near-adult children divorced, the father set up a corporation for his hardware store and residential rental business. He assigned to himself 51% of the shares, 20% to his son, 20% to his daughter, 6% to his general manager, and 3% to his secretary/bookkeeper (100% total). No actual money changed hands; no actual share certificates were issued; no shareholders ledger was kept. It was all an amicable family understanding.

Over the early years, the son and daughter took on increasingly active roles in the business. Thereupon, the 6% general manager's shares and the 3% secretary/bookkeeper's shares were "bought back" by the corporation. The father reassigned them equally to the son and daughter. At this point, each owned 24.5% of the business. The father still owned 51%. No shareholder meetings were ever held, nor were any minutes ever kept of this new ownership arrangement.

A few years later, the father suffered a massive stroke. He was paralyzed and unable to continue his leading role in the business. As his son had left the state to pursue his own profession (and had married), the father reassigned the shares as follows: 30% to himself, 50% to his daughter (who was then handling the business full time as general manager), and 20% to his son. The son understood this rearrangement and the reasons for it. But, no shareholder meeting was held; no revised shareholder records were kept; and nothing was in writing whatsoever.

Later, the father had a heart attack and died, quickly. There was no will or corporate resolution that addressed this situation. It was assumed that the son and daughter would inherit the father's 30% share of the business equally. This meant that the daughter would be 65% owner, and the son 35%. The brother and sister understood this, though, again, nothing was in writing.

During the probate process some 18 months later, the brother learned that the business and the personal residence of the father (which was in the corporation), was valued at nearly $2,000,000. The brother expected to own 35% of that amount or $700,000. But when the final accounting of the corporate estate was made, the brother owned only 15% of the business ($300,000), the sister owned 85% or $1,700,000. "How could this be?" the brother asked of his sister many times. He never get a satisfactory answer. The implication was that this was the father's wishes. But there was NOTHING IN WRITING to this effect!

Does the brother sue his sister for the $400,000 (700,000 – 300,000) that "disappeared"? If he does, what proof does he have that he owns 35% of the corporation after the father's death? Or, since no shareholders ledger or minutes of meetings were ever kept, does the brother sue for 50% of the business? The brother and sister had always been on good terms . . . until this point. This is the classical dilemma that all shareholders face in a closely held corporation when the patriarch dies. There is no documentary trail — no "clear and convincing evidence" — of what took place, when.

Inquiries the IRS Makes

When a closely held corporation is IRS selected for audit, the assigned agent submits to the controlling owner an *Information Document Request*: Form 4564. This is a two-page request which lists about 25 items wanted for examination. The first three items (usually) requested are—

1. The Shareholders Ledger,
2. The Minutes Book, and
3. The Articles of Incorporation

A bona fide corporation, if it shows a profit for the audit year (and/or for the year preceding and following) is supposed to declare and pay dividends. Accordingly, the IRS examiner checks the shareholders ledger (sometimes called: "stock book") to see if any dividends have ever been paid. If paid, the exact shareholder ownership percentages should be recomputed and posted up to the date of declaration of said dividends.

If no dividends have been declared, the IRS examiner reviews the minutes book to see if a shareholders' meeting was held to report and state why no dividends. If no meeting was held, the auditor looks at the net profit or net loss of the corporation's tax return. If a net profit, were the dividends treated as "loans" from the corporation without any documented payback obligation? Suspicions of tax evasion start racing through the auditor's mind. If a net loss, were the principal owners' salaries increased during the loss year? This raises other suspicions about self-dealings among the owners of the business.

The articles of incorporation and bylaws are IRS examined to see if there have been any amendments or changes — any at all — since the corporation was initially formed. If not, the auditor checks the bylaws for the boilerplate statement on *Compensation of Officers*. If such salaries are not stated, why were there no directors', shareholders', or other meetings designating the compensation to be paid to officers? If a compensation schedule is posted in the bylaws but never changed, do the current salaries reflect the schedule in the bylaws? If not, and if the salaries paid are higher than the boilerplate schedule, the excess salaries paid are prima facie treated by the IRS as *constructive dividends*.

If the IRS determines that dividends should have been declared, but were not, failure-to-declare-dividend penalties are imposed. Penalties for failure to report and pay tax on those dividends also are imposed. The penalties may be for ordinary negligence, or, if determined to be due to wilful intent, the 75% civil fraud penalty may be imposed. These penalties are assessed up front before any actual audit of the daily books of account begins.

At this point, the IRS has determined that the operation is **not** a bona fide corporation. It is an alter ego of the principals thereof. This means that the corporation's books will be audited with the objective of disallowing as personal expenditures of the owners many of the items which have been book entered as "business expenses."

2

ELECTION OF S STATUS

Becoming An S Corporation Is A TAX ELECTION Process: Not An Incorporation Process. Whether C Or S, The Business Is A Corporation And Must Conduct Its Affairs As Such. The S Status Election Requires IRS Form 2553 Whereon All Shareholders Must Consent UNANIMOUSLY. This Is More Achievable When There Are 15 Or Fewer Shareholders Than The 75 Maximum Allowable. A Valid S Election Can Be Revoked Voluntarily When 50% Or More Of The Total Shares Held Vote To Do So. Once S Status Is Revoked Or Otherwise Terminated, There Is A 5-Year Wait Period Before S Status Can Be Reelected.

When a small business entity incorporates under the General Corporation Law of any state, the IRS regards that entity, per se, as a C corporation. While most states recognize S corporations, there are no special provisions in state law to incorporate as such. There is a practical reason for this. The distinction between a C corporation and an S corporation is the TAX TREATMENT: **not** the incorporation treatment. Consequently, becoming an S corporation is a tax election by the shareholders of the incorporated entity. Those states which recognize S corporations for tax purposes follow the federal requirements for becoming an S.

A corporation which has no more than 75 shareholders *may elect* to become an S corporation. Upon such an election, the corporation itself is not subject to income tax, as in the case of a C corporation. Instead, the S corporation income is passed through and directly taxed to its shareholders. As a result, an S corporation becomes a *pass-through* entity much like that of a partnership.

The elective choice to be an S corporation is statutorily allowed in order to minimize the effect of taxation on deciding whether to be a corporation or a partnership. A corporation has limited liability. Thus, when electing to be an S corporation, shareholders get the tax benefits of a partnership along with the limited liability benefits of a corporation. This very special treatment applies only to small business corporations where the term "small" means 75 or fewer shareholders.

Accordingly, in this chapter we want to focus on the characteristics of an S corporation, how the election to become so is made, who are "eligible shareholders," and what happens when inadvertent termination of S status occurs. Whether the enterprise is "in" or "out" of S status, the corporate bona fides discussed in Chapter 1 are unaffected.

Subchapter S Overview

In case you may have wondered about it, where does the assignment of a "C" or "S" status come from? As indicated above, the distinction is not made under state law; it is made under federal tax law — the Internal Revenue Code — only.

The "C" comes from *Subchapter C*, whereas the "S" comes from *Subchapter S* of the Code. Both of these subchapters appear in Chapter 1 — Normal Taxes and Surtaxes, which appears in Subtitle A — Income Taxes, which appears in Title 26 — Internal Revenue Code of the United States Code (of *all* federal laws). Subchapter C is titled: *Corporate Distributions and Adjustments*. Correspondingly, Subchapter S is titled: *Tax Treatment of S Corporations and Their Shareholders*. In both of these subchapters, the tax treatment of each entity and its shareholders is of dominant concern. Now you know why we stressed the importance of a Shareholders Ledger and a Minutes Book, back in Chapter 1: Corporation Bona Fides.

Subchapter S of the IR Code spans Sections 1361 through 1379, some 14 sections in all. These 14 sections are arranged into four parts, which we identify in Figure 2.1. This figure gives you a good

U.S. CODE	Title 26 - INTERNAL REVENUE CODE	
Subtitle A - INCOME TAXES		
Chapter 1 - Normal Taxes and Surtaxes		
Subchapter S - Tax Treatment of S Corporation		
Section	Section Titles	Subsections
/////////	Part I - In General	/////////
1361	S Corporation Defined	(a) . . . (e)
1362	Election; Revocation; Termination	(a) . . . (g)
1363	Effect of Election on Corporation	(a) . . . (d)
/////////	Part II - Tax Treatment of Shareholders	/////////
1366	Pass-Thru of Items	(a) . . . (f)
1367	Adjustments to Stock Basis	(a) . . . (b)
1368	Distributions	(a) . . . (e)
/////////	Part III - Special Rules	/////////
1371	Coordination with Subchapter C	(a) . . . (e)
1372	Partnership Fringe Benefit Rules	(a) . . . (b)
1373	Foreign Income	(a) . . . (b)
1374	Tax on Built-in Gains	(a) . . . (e)
1375	Tax on Passive Investment Income	(a) . . . (d)
/////////	Part IV - Miscellaneous	/////////
1377	Definitions & Special Rule	(a) . . . (c)
1378	Taxable Year of S Corporation	(a) . . . (b)
1379	Transitional Rules on Enactment	(a) . . . (e)

Fig. 2.1 - Tax Code Sections Relating to S Corporation Status

overview of the contents of Subchapter S. In word count, the 14 Subchapter S sections comprise approximately 14,000 statutory words. This count *excludes* Treasury regulations, IRS rulings, and court rulings. It should be self-evident, therefore, that we can touch on only the highlights of Subchapter S in this and subsequent chapters hereto.

At this point, though, we do want to call your attention to Section 1371: *Coordination with Subchapter C*. Its subsection (a): *Application of Subchapter C Rules*, says—

Except as otherwise provided [in the Internal Revenue Code], *and except to the extent inconsistent with this subchapter, subchapter C shall apply to an S corporation and its shareholders.*

This makes it pretty clear to us that, from the point of view of general business management, there is no distinction between C and S types. Both are corporations and are expected to conduct their affairs as such. However, the corporation cannot be both a C and an S at the same time. It must be one type or the other.

Section 1371(b) makes the "one or the other" point clear by mandating that—

No carryover, and no carryback, arising for a taxable year for which a corporation is a C corporation may be carried to a taxable year for which such corporation is an S corporation.

This mandate gets us back to the point that the key C and S distinction is tax treatment. To keep the two tax treatments separate, separate tax returns must be filed. A C corporation files Form 1120, whereas an S corporation files Form 1120S. We'll discuss quite fully these two corporate tax forms in Chapter 3, next.

How S Status Defined

An S corporation is defined almost exclusively by its number and type of shareholders, rather than by its amount of capitalization, gross receipts, or business activities. The basic requisite is that it be a *domestic* corporation organized for profit purposes. Whenever there is profit made or loss sustained, there are tax accounting consequences. Nonprofit organizations, charitable organizations, and foreign organizations are just not eligible to become S corporations. Nor are financial institutions (banks and brokerage firms), insurance companies, or domestic international sales companies eligible.

The parameters of an S corporation are prescribed in Section 1361: *S Corporation Defined.* Subsection 1361(a)(1) says specifically—

*The term "S corporation" means, **with respect to any taxable year**, a small business corporation for which **an election** under section 1362(a) **is in effect** for such year.* [Emphasis added.]

As the emphasized terms imply, S status is a tax year to tax year affair. And, then, only after a shareholder election has been held. But let the election wane or become disqualified in some way, the entity reverts to a C corporation . . . automatically. So important is this concept of election status maintenance that we present a depiction of it in Figure 2.2. We also include other features of S status coming up shortly below.

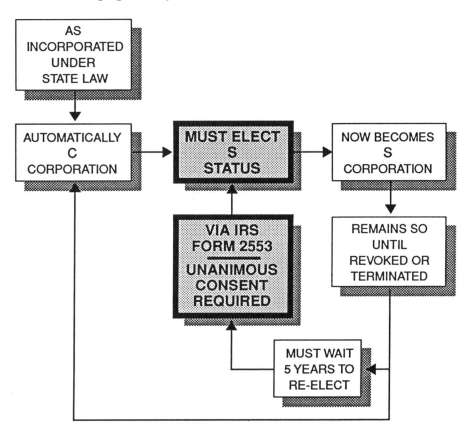

Fig. 2.2 - The "Tax Election" Relationship Between C and S Corporations

Subsection 1361(b)(1) supports the above by saying that a "small business corporation" means—

*a domestic corporation which is not an ineligible corporation and **which does not have**—*

(A)   more than 75 shareholders,
(B)   as a shareholder a person . . . who is not an individual,
(C)   a nonresident alien as a shareholder, and
(D)   more than 1 class of stock. [Be sure to read this clause as "not" more than.]

Partnerships and C corporations cannot be shareholders. However, certain trusts **can** be shareholders. Subsection 1361(c)(2)(A): ***Certain Trusts Permitted as Shareholders***, lists such trusts as—

(i)   A trust all of which . . . is owned by an individual who is a citizen or resident.
(ii)   A trust which . . . immediately before the death of the deemed owner continues in existence after such death, but only for a 2-year period . . .
(iii)   A trust with respect to stock transferred to it pursuant to the terms of a will, but only for a 2-year period . . .
(iv)   A trust created primarily to exercise the voting power of stock transferred to it.
(v)   An electing small business trust.

As you can sense from this listing, trusts can be complicating factors when counting the number of shareholders for the election of S status. The only unequivocal aspect is that a foreign trust cannot be a shareholder in an S corporation.

Counting the Shareholders

For most small and closely held corporations, the number of shareholders is not particularly significant. It rarely comes up to 75. But in highly touted and widely held small businesses expecting to grow big, the number 75 can be reached quite easily. This is especially true where there are a number of husband and wife owners, a number of trusts with multiple beneficiaries, and a new phenomenon called: Qualified Subchapter S Trusts (QSSTs). In these situations, how do you count the number of shareholders?

First off, subsection 1361(c)(1) says that—

a husband and wife (and their estates) shall be treated as 1 shareholder.

An "estate" comprises the assets of a deceased individual. It exists for a limited period of time (6 to 15 months) while the estate is being inventoried, appraised, and settled. At time of settlement, the assets (after debts and expenses are paid) are distributed either directly to individual heirs, or into a trust for piecemeal distributions to them.

So long as a husband and wife are married (whether they live together or not) at the time S status is voted upon, they count as one shareholder. If they become divorced, and each owns shares in the corporation, they are two shareholders. If the count was exactly 75 at the time of the election (when they were married), and they became divorced after the election, that would be 76 shareholders. Inadvertently, the S election becomes disqualified. This is a technicality which has to be astutely addressed by management. If, instead of a divorce, one of the spouses dies, the one shareholder count holds.

In the case of shares held in trust, the trust itself generally counts as one shareholder. This is especially true if there is only one current beneficiary of the trust. The trustee is the person who makes the election for or against S status.

If there are two or more current beneficiaries of a trust, and each is a substantial beneficial owner of the assets thereof (income and capital), a counting problem arises. Suppose, for example, that there are three current beneficiaries (A, B, and C) owning equally one-third of the trust. Is the trust treated as one shareholder, or is it treated as three shareholders?

Answer: It depends. If the books of account were set up as subtrust A, subtrust B, and subtrust C, and separate trust tax returns were filed for the year of the election, a case could be made that there were three shareholders: not one. There would be a problem, though, if one of the three beneficiaries disapproved of the S status election. As you'll see below, he alone would have veto power over 74 other shareholders who might approve of the S election. Allowing any one person veto power can cause endless acrimony and lawsuits.

Unanimous Consent Required

Section 1362 is titled: *Election; Revocation; Termination* [of S status]. Approximately 2,800 tax law words are used. At the moment, our concern is the election process under subsection (a). This subsection reads in full, as follows:

(1)   *Except as provided in subsection (g)* [re the 5-year wait period after termination], *a small business corporation may elect, in accordance with the provision of this section, to be an S corporation.*

(2)   *An election under this subsection shall be valid **only if all** persons who are **shareholders** in such corporation on the day on which the election is made **consent to such election**.* [Emphasis added.]

In other words, unanimous consent must be attained on the date of the election. This can be a Herculean task when there are 15, 35, 50 or more shareholders involved. Controversies can erupt because of differences in tax interests. A high income shareholder may not want any S corporation profits passed through to him, though he probably would want the losses to pass through. Conversely, a low income shareholder would certainly want the profits passed through, but not the losses.

To minimize shareholder controversy concerning their own individual taxes, it is best to seek S status when there are 15 or fewer shareholders involved. Section 1362(a) requires unanimous consent only "on the day which" the election is made. Once an S election is valid, new shareholders are not required to consent to the election. Nor can they terminate an election by objecting to it, or by refusing to accept its pass-through tax treatment.

At the time of the election, each eligible shareholder must read and sign (and date) the following IRS-prepared consent statement:

Under penalties of perjury, we declare that we consent to the election of the above-named corporation to be an S corporation under section 1362(a) and that we have examined this consent statement, including accompanying schedules and statements, and to the best of our knowledge and belief, it is true, correct, and complete. **We understand that our consent is binding and may not be withdrawn after the corporation has made a valid election.** [Emphasis added.]

/s/	(date)
/s/	(date)
/s/	(date)
etc.	etc.

Timing of the Election

Section 1362(b): **When Made**, designates the time frame within which a valid election can be made. Fundamentally, there are just two options. These are—

(A)   at any time during the preceding taxable year, **or**

(B)   at any time during the [current] *taxable year* [but so long as] *on or before the 15th day of the 3rd month of the taxable year.* [2^{1}/2 months].

The advantage of option (A) is that it gives the shareholders time to discuss the impact of the election on their individual tax returns, without being under pressure. In the meantime, the business operates as a C corporation, and when doing so, has to establish a "taxable year." This can be a calendar year (January through December) or a fiscal year (starting any month and ending 12 months later). Because individuals are on a calendar year basis, their S election should also be on a calendar year.

The disadvantage of option (A) is that, should the business operate as a C corporation for a year or more, there are transition accounting adjustments when switching to S status. These adjustments pertain to: (a) accumulated earnings, (b) built-in gains, (c) investment credits, and (d) inventory recapture (if any).

The advantage of option (B) is that the founders can form the corporation and get right into the election process during the first $2^{1/2}$ months of the first year of operation. This avoids the fiscal versus calendar year issue, and the transitional tax adjustments.

The disadvantage of option (B) is that it places a time constraint ($2^{1/2}$ months) on shareholders who may not have worked with each other before. There can be cause for confusion and doubt, rather than consensus. During the entire $2^{1/2}$-month period, there must be no ineligible shareholders, and the entity itself must not be ineligible. Although the IRS has authority under subsection (b)(5) to accept late elections after the $2^{1/2}$ month period, its conditions for acceptance are rather stringent. Otherwise, a late election reverts to option (A).

We summarize the above for you in Figure 2.3. If S status is desired in the very first year of business operation, it is best to educate the shareholders and get the business started, the moment it is legally incorporated.

Once the election is valid, it—

*shall be effective for the taxable year of the corporation for which it is made, and for **all succeeding taxable years** of the corporation, until such election is terminated under subsection (d)* [subsec. 1362(c)]. [Emphasis added.]

Elect on Form 2553

As you would expect, there is a special IRS form for making the S status election. It is Form 2553: *Election by Small Business Corporation*. Although arranged in three parts, it is Part I: *Election Information*, that is most pertinent here. The form is accompanied

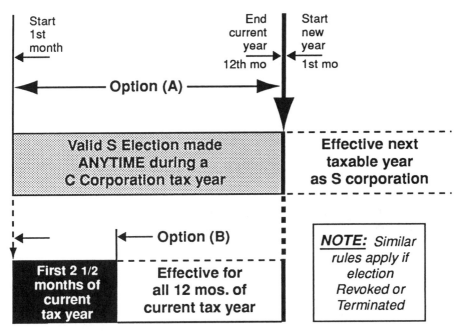

Fig. 2.3 - Options When S Election Becomes Effective

by approximately 3,600 words of instructions. Completing the form is serious tax legal business. Because so, each shareholder should be given a blank copy of Form 2553 (front and back) before seeking his/her signature on it.

As partly edited, preprinted headnotes on Form 2553 read:

1. *This election to be an S corporation can be accepted **only if all** [8] tests are met under **Who May Elect** on page 1 of the instructions. All signatures* [must be] *originals (no photocopies).*

2. *Do not file* [a tax return] *for an S corporation for any year before the election takes effect.*

3. *If the corporation was in existence before the effective date of this election, see **Taxes an S Corporation May Owe** [in] the instructions.*

The required Election Information in Part I is entered onto 14 alphabetized lines and columns. For instructional overview, we list the captions of these 14 entry items:

A. Employer identification number
B. Date incorporated
C. State of incorporation
D. Effective tax year of election
E. Name of person for IRS contact
F. Phone number for IRS contact
G. If corporation name/address change, ☐
H. Earliest of 3 dates if election is for first year of operation
I. Selected taxable year (If other than a calendar year, complete Part II.)
J. Name/address each shareholder
K. Shareholders' consent statement
L. Number of shares; date acquired
M. Shareholders' Tax IDs
N. End of each shareholder's tax year

Items J, K, L, M, and N are columnized. This is because there is a separate line for five entries for each shareholder. The preprinted form accommodates only five shareholders. The instructions tell you to attach a *continuation sheet* (or sheets) to accommodate **all** eligible shareholders. Again, all must sign and date and indicate the number of shares each holds.

For shareholder familiarization purposes, the general format of Form 2553 is presented in Figure 2.4. Although the instructions do not require so, we think it a good idea for every signing shareholder to receive a photocopy of the election form, once it is certified by a responsible officer of the corporation. A requirement to do so could be specified in the bylaws, thereby avoiding subsequent controversy.

Upon attaining unanimous consents, and authentication by a responsible officer — the President or Secretary, usually — the election form is sent to the IRS Service Center designated in the instructions. It is sent solo (including continuation sheets): without any other tax forms attached.

FORM 2553	ELECTION BY SMALL BUSINESS CORPORATION - Under Sec. 1362 of IR Code				
3 Headnotes: See Text					
Part I ELECTION INFORMATION					

Corporation Name, Address, City, State, ZIP		**A**	EIN
		B	Date incorporated
		C	State of incorporation

D	Tax year for which election effective		_mo_ _dy_ _yr_
E	Name, address of person to contact	**F**	Phone number
G	Change of name or address after applying for EIN ▶ ☐		
H	If effective 1st year of operation, enter **earliest date of:** (1) 1st shareholders, (2) 1st assets, or (3) 1st business _mo_ _dy_ _yr_		
I	Select tax year: Ending month _____ - if other than calendar year, complete Part II		

J	K		L		M	N
Name, address each shareholder	**CONSENT STATEMENT**		Shares held		SSN each s/h	Each s/h tax year ends
	signature	date	number	date		
Use Continuation Sheets as Needed						

Authenticating Officer	signature	title	date

Part II	Selection of Fiscal Tax Year
Part III	Qualified Subchapter S Trust Election

Fig. 2.4 - General Contents of Form 2553 : Election of S Status

Revocation by Majority Vote

An S status election by means of Form 2553 is not forever cast in concrete. It can be revoked voluntarily by those shareholders with more than 50 percent of the total shares issued and outstanding.

On this point, subsection 1362(d)(1): *Termination by Revocation*, says—

An election under subsection (a) may be terminated by revocation . . . [but] only if shareholders holding more than one-half of the shares of stock of the corporation on the day on which the revocation is made consent to the revocation.

To revoke an election, the S corporation must file a Statement of Revocation with the IRS service center where Form 2553 was initially filed. There is no preprinted statement-of-revocation form. The authenticating officer of the corporation who will sign the statement ("under penalties of perjury") should review Regulation § 1.1362-6(A)(3): **Revocation of S election**, and Regulation § 1.1362-6(b)(1): *Manner of shareholders' consents*. The essence of these two regulations is to "reverse" the tax legal words of Form 2553 and to show the exact count of all shares outstanding, non-voting as well as voting. If more appropriate, the corporation's Election Statement and the shareholders' Consent Statement may be two separate documents attached together as one Statement of Revocation.

Once the revocation is validated by an authenticating officer of the corporation, its **effective date** is—

(i) the 1st day of the taxable year . . . if a revocation is made during the taxable year and **on or before** the 15th day of the 3rd month thereof, and

(ii) the 1st day of the following taxable year . . . if a revocation is made during the taxable year **but after** such 15th day. [Emphasis added.]

In other words, the effective date of a revocation is comparable to that when the S-status election was validated (recall Fig. 2.3). Additionally, however, the revocation may specify a prospective date of the corporation's own choosing [Sec. 1362(d)(1)(D)]. If the revocation specifies a date other than the first day of a tax year, a "split tax year" results. The split tax will create an S short year and a C short year. This adds transition-year complications due to *pro rata allocations* because of the different tax treatment between C and S corporations [Sec. 1362(e)(1)-(6)].

Revocation is a voluntary termination of the S status election. There are other situations where termination may be involuntary or inadvertent. The two most common reasons are subsection (d)(2): *By corporation ceasing to be a small business corporation*, and subsection (d)(3): *Where passive investment income exceeds 25 percent of gross receipts for 3 consecutive taxable years and corporation has accumulated earnings and profits.*

Passive investment income includes gross receipts derived from rents, royalties, interest, dividends, annuities, and gain from sales or exchanges of stock or securities in publicly traded C corporations. The term "passive investment income" does **not** include that derived from *the active conduct of a trade or business*, whether in C or S form. We'll have more to say on passive income when we get to personal service corporations (Sec. 269A), corporations subject to accumulated earnings tax (Sec. 531), and personal holding companies (Secs. 541–547) in Chapter 8.

Reinstatement after Termination

Once a valid S corporation election is terminated or revoked, the corporation or any successor corporation is prohibited (generally) from making a new election for five years. This is so prescribed by Section 1362(a): *Election after Termination*. The 5-year period begins with the tax year *after* the first tax year for which a termination or revocation is effective. The purpose of this 5-year prohibition is to discourage using the election-revocation-reelection option for "pumping" tax benefits back and forth between C and S status. Personal gain can be accelerated this way. Motivation for such usually comes from the dominant shareholders. The "back and forth" also can be done circumventively by creating successor corporations. Under Section 1362(g), a successor corporation is treated as the same corporation whose S status was terminated.

A successor corporation is one in which 50 percent or more of the stock is owned, directly or indirectly, by the same shareholders who owned 50 percent or more of the stock of the old corporation. It is also a corporation which acquires a substantial portion (over 50 percent) of the assets which are, or were, assets of the old corporation. However, in the past, the IRS has ruled that a C corporation which purchased all of the stock of an S corporation, and later liquidated the S corporation to acquire its assets, was not considered a successor corporation. In cases like this, the acquiring C corporation can itself elect S corporation status *without* waiting five years to do so.

There is a relief clause in Section 1362(g) which can soften the 5-year waiting period. The particular clause is . . . *unless the IRS consents to such election* [before the lapse of 5 years]. To get such relief, the corporation seeking reelection of S status must satisfy the IRS that, for good cause shown, its consent should be granted [Reg. § 1.1362-5(a)]. One of the best chances of this is proving that the termination was inadvertent and not part of a planned election to terminate. Also, if, after termination, it can be shown that more than 50% of the shares were owned by persons who were *not* shareholders on the date of termination — they were "newcomers" to the enterprise — the IRS would likely be persuaded. Other consent examples would be where the revocation of S status was withdrawn before it took effect, or the revocation itself was invalid. A revocation is invalid if an ineligible shareholder participates in the election or if the corporation itself is ineligible (such as not being in the *active conduct* of a trade or business).

The primary benefit of S status is that the business — being permitted to have up to 75 shareholders — can raise significantly more capital than a closely held C corporation with 10 or fewer shareholders. Being capital short year after year, as many close corporations are, induces the controlling interests to distort the accounting process . . . often for their own personal gain.

3

FORMS 1120 AND 1120S

Corporations, Whether C Or S, Have To File Tax Returns Every Year Of Their Legal Lives. For C Corporations Form 1120 Applies; For S Corporations Form 1120S Is Used. Each Is A 4-Page Form, Plus Various Attachments. All INCOME And DEDUCTIONS Are Displayed On Page 1 Whereas Financial Results (ASSETS And LIABILITIES) Appear On Page 4. For C Corporations, Cost of Goods, Compensation Of Officers, And Computation Of Tax Are Shown On Pages 2 And 3. For S Corporations, Page 2 Consists Of General Information And Page 3 Consists Of "Distributive Share" Items That Pass Through To Shareholders.

Form 1120 is the tax return for a C corporation; Form 1120S is the tax return for an S corporation. Form 1120 is titled: *U.S. Corporation Income Tax Return*. Form 1120S is titled: *U.S. Income Tax Return for an S Corporation*. A bold printed instruction below this 1120S title reads:

Do not file this form unless the corporation has timely filed Form 2553 to elect to be an S corporation.

The implication from this instruction is that when in doubt about S corporation status, the responsible officer must file Form 1120 as a C corporation.

A headnote on both Forms 1120 and 1120S refers the responsible officer to each form's "separate instructions." The

Form 1120 instructions consist of 15 pages of 3-columnar text comprising about 27,000 words. The Form 1120S instructions consist of 25 pages comprising some 45,000 words. The implication here is that Form 1120S is more complicated than Form 1120. The reason, of course, is the tax feature of passing through certain income, deductions, and credits from the S corporation to its S shareholders.

As having separate instructions indicates, there are differences between Forms 1120 and 1120S. There are also differences between Forms 1120/1120S and each shareholder's own individual tax return: Form 1040. Consequently, what we want to do in this chapter is to point out the differences between Forms 1120 and 1120S in a useful and instructional way. By "useful," we mean that you will be sufficiently informed of the structural elements of a corporation's tax return. By having this knowledge, you will not confuse, commingle, or overlap corporate tax matters with your own personal income tax return. As we pointed out previously, shareholders in small and closely held corporations tend to "alter ego" their corporate and personal returns together. This can lead to unpleasant surprises when the IRS applies corporate tax accounting rules which differ markedly from personal tax accounting. Our first instructional effort in this regard is to familiarize you with the similarities and differences between Forms 1120 and 1120S.

Introductory Differences

Both sets of instructions to Forms 1120/1120S have an introductory section title: *General Information; Who Must File*. For a C corporation, the "who must file" reads (in pertinent part)—

*Unless exempt . . . , all domestic corporations (including corporations in bankruptcy) must file **whether or not** they have taxable income. Domestic corporations must file Form 1120 . . . **unless** they are required to file* [otherwise]. [Emphasis added.]

Thus, the first rule of corporate engagement is that a tax return MUST BE FILED. This is so whether the corporation makes a profit, sustains a loss, is solvent, or insolvent. This same "must file" mandate applies to S corporations.

The S corporation instructions on "who must file" read:

*A corporation must file Form 1120S if, (a) it elected to be an S corporation by filing Form 2553, (b) the IRS accepted the election, and (c) the election remains in effect. **Do not** file Form 1120S for any tax year before the year the election takes effect.*

Thus, if you are not a duly elected S corporation, you are a C corporation. You file Form 1120. The 1120 can be used for a wide range of business activities from \$100,000 (0.1 million) to \$100,000,000 (100 million) . . . or more. The only limitation of concern is that the stock shares are privately held, and are restricted to such. Once corporate stock is federally and state registered for public offerings, the designation "small" or "close" no longer holds.

For the purpose of comparing Forms 1120 and 1120S, we will use the term "block" where the return does not have a caption labeled "Schedule" or "Part." On page 1, particularly, the various line entries are horizontally ruled in information groups or blocks. As we compare the entry blocks, the understanding is that where we do not point out the C and S differences, the required entry information is the same.

At the top of page 1, there is a body of information that we call: *Identification Block*. It requires the name and address of the corporation, the EIN (Employer Identification Number), date incorporated, and total assets. In addition, there are two sets of checkboxes: a vertical grouping on the left side and a horizontal grouping across the whole page.

The vertical groupings compare as follows:

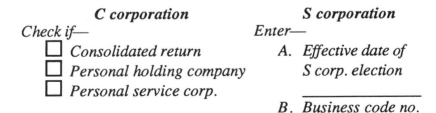

C corporation	S corporation
Check if—	*Enter—*
☐ *Consolidated return*	A. *Effective date of*
☐ *Personal holding company*	*S corp. election*
☐ *Personal service corp.*	_____
	B. *Business code no.*
	_____

A C corporation can be an umbrella entity for a number of other C corporations as subsidiaries. If so elected by the parent company, one return — a "consolidated return" — can be presented for all.

The horizontal grouping of checkboxes carries the instruction: *Check applicable box—*

C corp: ☐ *Initial return* ☐ *Final return* ☐ *Change of address*
S corp: ☐ *Initial return* ☐ *Final return* ☐ *Change of address*
☐ *Amended return*
Enter number of shareholders at end of tax year ▶ _____

As you'll note, there is no "Amended return" checkbox for a C corporation. This is because a special form is available for such purpose, namely: Form 1120X: *Amended U.S. Corporation Income Tax Return*. If an S corporation has to amend its return, it refiles Form 1120S and X-marks the indicated checkbox.

Every S corporation has to enter in the Identification Block its end-of-year number of shareholders. (A C corporation does not have to do this.) The reason for this is that each shareholder is issued a separate Schedule K-1 (Form 1120S): *Shareholder's Share of Income, Credits, Deductions, etc.,* by the corporation. The K-1 is issued every year, whether dividends are paid or not. A C corporation issues Form 1099-DIV: *Dividends and Distributions* only when dividends are declared.

At the bottom of page 1 of Forms 1120 and 1120S, there is a signature block. The nomenclature and the jurat cause (*under penalties of perjury . . .*) are identical on both forms. A responsible officer of the corporation must personally sign, date, and include his or her title.

Income & Deduction Blocks

The key operating results of corporate activities are displayed in two principal entry blocks which take up most of the front page of Forms 1120 and 1120S. One is the *Income* block; the other is the *Deductions* block. The total income minus total deductions produces net earnings or net loss. This is what both forms are all about. Once the net income or loss is established, the tax treatment thereof differs markedly between C and S corporations.

To give you an overview of what items of income and what items of deductions appear on the forms, we present Figure 3.1. We use the C form for reference purposes, as it is the fallback return should the S status not be effective. We show blank lines on the S form column where the C items do not apply.

Glancing at the income portion of Figure 3.1, what is the first thing that jumps out at you?

In the S form column, there are five blank lines. These are: (a) dividends, (b) interest, (c) rents, (d) royalties, and (e) capital gains. Why are these income items not on Form 1120S?

Answer: Said five items are passed through for taxing at the individual shareholder level. In a C corporation case, these five items are taxed at the corporation level. Both C and S corporations may generate said income; it is just that they are taxed differently.

This time, glance at the deductions portion of Figure 3.1. The only significant difference is the line for charitable contributions. Whereas a C corporation can deduct against income up to 10% of its net earnings as contributions to charity, an S corporation cannot do so. If the S corporation does make a charitable contribution, the deduction benefit is passed through to its shareholders. An individual shareholder can deduct up to 50% of his gross income for charitable contributions.

The real tax difference between Forms 1120 and 1120S is the last line in Figure 3.1. For a C corporation, the net line (income minus deductions: line 28) is called: *Taxable income.* This is because it is taxable to the corporation; it is not passed through to the shareholders.

In contrast, the net line (21 in Figure 3.1) for an S corporation is called: *Ordinary income.* Whether it is income (positive) or loss (negative), it is passed through to all S corporation shareholders in proportion to each shareholder's ownership interests.

Pages 2 and 3 Compared

Sharp differences appear on pages 2 and 3 of Forms 1120 and 1120S. On the 1120, there are five preprinted schedules; on the

SMALL C & S CORPORATIONS

FORM 1120	Page 1 of Corporation Returns	FORM 1120S
INCOME		
1	Gross receipts **LESS** returns & allowances	1
2	Cost of goods sold	2
3	Gross profit [subtract line 2 from line 1]	3
4	Dividends	/////
5	Interest	/////
6	Gross rents	/////
7	Gross royalties	/////
8	Capital gain net income	/////
9	Net gain or loss: Form 4797	4
10	Other income	5
11	**TOTAL INCOME [ADD the above]**	6
DEDUCTIONS		
12	Compensation of officers	7
13	Salaries & wages	8
14	Repairs & maintenance	9
15	Bad debts	10
16	Rents	11
17	Taxes & licenses	12
18	Interest	13
19	Charitable contributions	/////
20 /////	Depreciation : Form 4562	/////
21	LESS depreciation claimed elsewhere	14
22	Depletion	15
23	Advertising	16
24	Pension and profit sharing plans	17
25	Employee benefit programs	18
26	Other deductions [Attach schedule]	19
27	**TOTAL DEDUCTIONS [ADD the above]**	20
/////	**SUBTRACT TOTAL DEDUCTIONS FROM TOTAL INCOME**	/////
28	TAXABLE INCOME ⊠ ORDINARY INCOME	21

Fig. 3.1 - Comparison of Income & Deduction Items on Forms 1120 & 1120S

1120S there are three such schedules. The titles and overall arrangement of these various schedules are presented in Figure 3.2.

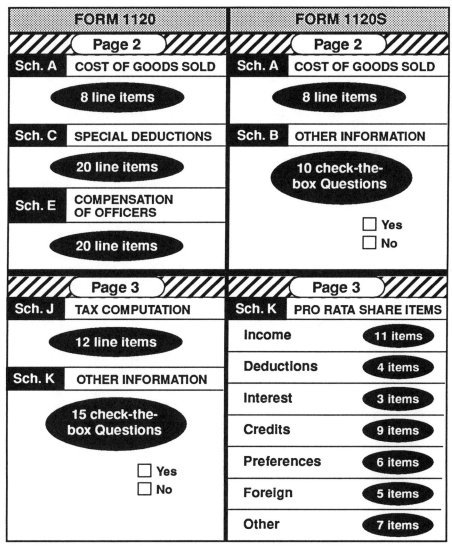

Fig. 3.2 - Contents of Pages 2 and 3 of Forms 1120 and 1120S

Schedule A (which is the first entry block on page 2 of both forms) is titled: *Cost of Goods Sold.* It consists of eight lines for dollar entries, nine checkboxes, plus one percentage entry line (re the LIFO method of inventory). The Schedules A on both forms are *identical*. The "cost of goods" information from this schedule enters directly onto line 2 of both forms (as per Figure 3.1).

As you can note in Figure 3.2, there is no Schedule B on Form 1120, as there is on Form 1120S: *Other Information*. However, Schedule K on Form 1120 is similarly titled. The information sought has to do with such matters as method of accounting, principal business, product or service, affiliation (if any) with other corporations, foreign financial accounts, and numerous other check-the-box type questions.

Also note that Form 1120 contains Schedules C, E, and J for which there are no corresponding schedules on Form 1120S. Schedule C: *Dividends and Special Deductions*, is a truly unique C corporation benefit. This is a special deduction varying from 42% to 100% of the dividends received from 12 different types of corporations (domestic and foreign) in which the filing corporation is a purely passive investor. The rationale for this deduction is the fact that any dividends declared by the filing C corporation is "double taxed": once at the corporate level and again at the shareholder level.

Schedule E (Form 1120): *Compensation of Officers*, requires listing the names and compensation amount of the five highest paid officers of the C corporation. In addition, Schedule E requires a showing of:

(a)   *Social security number*
(b)   *Percent of time devoted to business*
(c)   *Percent of corporation stock owned*

It is not that this same information cannot be asked of S corporation officers. It is just that C corporations lend themselves more readily to five or fewer officers owning 50% or more of the stock, and thereby controlling 100% of the business. By having the officers' names and compensation posted where they can be seen at a glance, the IRS has a quick target for inquiry when Form 1120 is audit examined. As you'll see in the next chapter, the IRS applies certain "tests" for reasonableness of officer compensation.

For the moment, we'll skip over Schedule J (Form 1120): *Tax Computation*. What we haven't explained thus far is that there is a partial tax on S corporations. We want to discuss both the C and S corporate taxes in a comparative way. To do this, we need to tell about how C and S corporations treat capital gains and losses.

Capital Gains & Losses

Corporations, like individuals, can hold assets which, when sold or exchanged, can generate net capital gains or net capital losses. The common schedule for reporting these transactions is Schedule D: *Capital Gains and Losses*. There is a Schedule D/1040 for individuals, a Schedule D/1041 for trusts, a Schedule D/1065 for partnerships, a Schedule D/1120 for C corporations, and a Schedule D/1120S for S corporations. It is the Schedules D for Form 1120 and Form 1120S that we want to compare here.

Schedule D/1120 consists of three parts, namely:

Part I — Short-Term Capital Gains and Losses (S/T)
• Assets Held One Year or Less

Part II — Long-Term Capital Gains and Losses (L/T)
• Assets Held More Than One Year

Part III — Summary of Parts I and II

Part III of D/1120 consists of just three lines, to wit:

1. Excess of S/T capital gain over L/T capital loss _____
2. Excess of L/T capital gain over S/T capital loss _____
3. *Net capital gain income*. Add lines 1 and 2 _____
   • Enter line 3 on page 1 of Form 1120 at
     line 8 (in Figure 3.1)

Only the net capital gain of a C corporation goes into income. What happens if, instead of net capital gain, there is a net capital loss for a C corporation?
Answer: The instructions say—

Capital losses are allowed only to the extent of capital gains. A net capital loss is carried back 3 years and carried forward 5 years as a short-term capital loss.

There is a separate line in Part I of Schedule D/1120 to accommodate the capital loss carryback/carryforward. It is captioned: *Unused capital loss carryover (attach computation).*

Now, what about Schedule D for Form 1120S? Its caption is: **Capital Gains and Losses and Built-in Gains.** Do note this add-on portion: *Built-in Gains.* For S corporations **before 1987**, there is a capital gains tax; for S corporations **after 1986** there is a built-in gains tax. The capital gains tax portion is computed in Part III; the built-in gains tax is computed in Part IV of Schedule D/1120S. For our purposes, Part III would not likely apply, though Part IV could apply. If an after-1986 S corporation started out as an S, and had never lapsed into a C, Part IV would not likely apply.

Schedule D, Form 1120S consists of four parts, namely:

Part I   — Same as Form 1120, except that there is an offset (negative) entry for: *Tax on **short-term** capital gain included* [in Part IV].

Part II   — Same as Form 1120, except that there is an offset (negative) entry for: *Tax on **long-term** capital gain included* [in Parts III and IV].

Part III — Capital Gains Tax (12 entry lines)

Part IV — Built-in Gains Tax (8 entry lines)

The overall net effect is that there is a potential built-in gains tax on S corporations. After adjustments and subtractions, the rate of tax is 35%. This tax is designed to prevent C corporations from converting to S status, then passing through any retained nontaxable/built-in corporate gains to shareholders who have a lower individual rate than 35%. Once the built-in gains are taxed at the S level, any *excess* capital gains or losses are indeed passed through to shareholders.

How Tax Items Compare

In Figure 3.1, the last line there for a C corporation is line 28: *Taxable Income* (or loss). Correspondingly, the last line for an S corporation is line 21: *Ordinary Income* (or loss). For an S corporation, the next line that follows is line 22: *Tax*. The entry amount is the sum of three sublines, namely:

22a — *Excess net passive income tax*
22b — *Tax from Schedule D (Form 1120S)*
22c — *Certain recapture and look-back tax*

All three of these items relate to transitions from C status to S status. Where there is or has been a transition, the official instructions to these sublines must be studied. Otherwise, if the corporation has always been an S corporation, lines 22a, b, and c do not apply.

The tax items for a C corporation are quite a different matter from those above. In the first place, although we labeled line 28 in Figure 3.1 as "Taxable income," there are actually **two** taxable incomes on Form 1120. There is one *before* and one *after*. The official sequence is as follows:

28. *Taxable income **before** net operating loss and special dividend deductions*
29. **Less:** *a. Net operating loss deduction*
        b. Special dividends received deduction
        c. Add lines 29a and 29b
30. *Taxable income. Subtract line 29c from line 28*
31. *Total tax (from Schedule J)*

Schedule J of Form 1120 is titled: *Tax Computation (see instructions)*. The instructions are much too complex for any meaningful presentation here. Instead, we are going to edit and abbreviate Schedule J and present it to you as Figure 3.3. We simply want to list the tax items involved. For closely held C corporations which do not lapse into personal service corporations or personal holding companies, Schedule J is not too formidable.

Note that the last line in Figure 3.3 is captioned: *Total tax.* The preprinted instructions on Schedule J direct the total tax amount onto line 31 shown above.

Schedule J	Form 1120	Tax Computation		
1	☐ Member of controlled group; use tax worksheet			
2	☐ Personal service corporation; use 35% rate			
3	**Income tax :** All others, use rate schedule			
4	Foreign tax credit	a		///////
	Possessions tax credit	b		///////
	Nonconventional fuel credit	c		///////
	General business credit	d		///////
	Credit for prior year minimum tax	e		///////
5	**Total credits:** Add the above ▶			
6	Subtract line 5 from line 3			
7	Personal holding company tax			
8	Recapture taxes			
9	Alternative minimum tax			
10	Add lines 6 through 9			
11	Public school board credit			
12	**Total tax:** Subtract line 11 from line 10			
///	• Enter line 12 on page 1 at line 31 of Form 1120 (see text).			
	NOTE: At line 4, there are **19** credit possibilities, each of which requires a separate computational form of its own.			

Fig. 3.3 - Edited Content of Schedule J for C Corporation Tax

How Tax Rates Compare

A C corporation is taxed independently of its shareholders. Unlike individual shareholders who may file under one of five different filing statuses (single, married joint, married separate, head of household, qualifying widow(er)), a corporation has only one filing status. Though not expressly so designated, a corporation can be thought of as a single person. As a result, just one tax rate schedule applies.

Although there is just one "schedule," up to eight different tax rates apply. There are five such tax rates for individuals. We display these rates side by side in Figure 3.4. The dollar amounts displayed represent the "end of the bracket" for the tax rate shown. The displayed rates are called: *ordinary tax rates*. These rates apply to taxable income only. There are also capital gain tax rates, special tax rates, and alternative minimum tax rates.

C CORPORATIONS		INDIVIDUALS		
Tax Rate	Taxable Income	Tax Rate	Taxable Income	
			Single	Married
15%	to $50,000	15%	to $26,000	to $43,000
25%	to $75,000	28%	to $62,000	to $104,000
34%	to $100,000	31%	to $130,000	to $159,000
39%	to $335,000	36%	to $283,000	to $283,000
34%	to $10,000,000	39.6%	over $283,000	over $283,000
35%	to $15,000,000	NOTE: The above dollar amounts are "rounded" for 1999. Individual amounts are indexed for inflation.		
30%	to $18,333,333			
35%	over $18,333,333			

S CORPORATIONS	INDIVIDUALS
Capital gains rate: 35%	Capital gains rate: 20%

Fig. 3.4 - Tax Rates: Corporations vs. Individuals

Glancing at Figure 3.4, what do you notice?

First, except for the 15% bracket, there is no parallelism in the rate structure between C corporations and individuals. Yes, both have graduated rates but the graduations are nonuniform. They are hodgepodge (politics, no doubt). Why not 15%, 25%, 30%, 35%, 40%, or 15%, 20%, 25%, 30%, 35%?

The second thing you may notice in Figure 3.4 is that the maximum tax rate for individuals is 39.6% for taxable incomes over about $300,000. For C corporations, a 39% rate applies to taxable incomes over about $335,000. The intent, as we understand it, is to put individuals on a par with corporations in the taxable income range of $300,000 to $350,000. The idea is to de-incentivetize individuals from forming C corporations just to take advantage of tax rate differentials and other tax benefits that might apply.

The third thing you may notice in Figure 3.4 is that for C corporations over $18,000,000 or so, the tax rate is a flat 35%. The 35% rate is a "pegging target" for flat taxing all types of corporate activities where graduated rates do not apply. The best example of this 35% pegging is an S corporation. For S corporations, the ordinary (graduated) rates do not apply. Said corporations are taxed primarily on their built-in capital gains (if any). After certain adjustments, a flat 35% rate applies. We indicate this in the lower portion of Figure 3.4. The same flat rate concept applies to personal service corporations, personal holding companies, controlled corporate groups, and other corporation special tax matters.

Schedule K-1 (Form 1120S)

As indicated above, S corporations are not subject to ordinary income tax rates. Thus, if an S corporation generates positive net income, what happens? Answer: The income and other items are passed through *pro rata* to all shareholders. How is this done? Answer: With Schedule K-1 (Form 1120S).

The Schedule K-1 is titled: *Shareholder's Share of Income, Credits, Deductions, etc.* The left half of the identification block displays each shareholder's name, address, ZIP code, and Tax ID (social security number). The right half displays the corporation's name, address, ZIP code and Tax ID (employer identification number). There is a **separate** Schedule K-1 issued to and for each shareholder of record at the close of the corporation's tax year.

As a reminder of this, on page 1 of Form 1120S, the last item in the identification block states:

Enter number of shareholders in the corporation at end of the tax year ▶ _____.

If, for example, the number 17 is entered, the IRS would expect to see 17 Schedules K-1 attached to Form 1120S. The IRS uses the K-1 information to computer cross-check what each shareholder reports on his own Form 1040 return.

Schedule K-1 (Form 1120S)	SHAREHOLDER'S SHARE OF INCOME, CREDITS, DEDUCTIONS, ETC.	Tax Year
Shareholder's Identification	Corporation's Identification	
A. % stock ownership B. IRS Center	C. Tax shelter registration D. ☐ Amended ☐ Final	

(a) Pro rata share items	(b) Amount	(c) Where to enter
INCOME (LOSS) — 11 items		
DEDUCTIONS — 4 items		
INVESTMENT INTEREST — 3 items		
CREDITS — 9 items		
ADJUSTMENTS & PREFERENCES — 6 items		
FOREIGN TAXES — 5 items		
OTHER — 8 items		
SUPPLEMENTAL INFORMATION (14 blank lines)		

Fig. 3.5 - General Format & Contents of Schedule K-1 (Form 1120S)

For overview instructional purposes, we present in Figure 3.5 the general format and contents of Schedule K-1. Not readily self-evident in this figure is that there are 46 captioned lines for entering pro rata share information. There is also a 47th line (consisting of 14 blank lines) labeled: *Supplemental Information.* Obviously, we are not going to explain all 47 of the K-1 lines. However, we do group them into functional blocks as they officially appear. Column (c) directs the shareholders where to enter on their Forms 1040.

Particularly note in Figure 3.5 item A: % stock ownership. The official caption to this item reads—

> A. *Shareholder's percentage of stock ownership **for the tax year** (see instructions)* ▶ _____%.

The instructions read:

> *If there was a change in* [the number of] *shareholders or in the relative interest in stock the shareholders owned during the tax year, each shareholder's percentage of ownership is **weighted for the number of days in the tax year** that stock was owned.* [Emphasis added.]

In other words, you have to think in terms of **shareholder days** of ownership throughout the year. If, for example, there were two shareholders each owning 15% of the stock at the end of the year, one holding it for 146 days (40% of the year) and the other holding it for 365 days, the 146-day owner would have a 6% (15% x 40%) ownership interest for the tax year.

Once you figure each shareholder's percentage of ownership for the year, you cross check your computations by adding all individual percentages to total 100%. Then you multiply each dollar amount in Schedule K (NOT K-1) by each shareholder's percentage (item A). You enter the result in Schedule K-1.

Where did Schedule K come from? We displayed it to you in Figure 3.2 (as page 3 of Form 1120S), but did not call your attention to it. This schedule is officially titled: *Shareholders' Shares of Income, Credits, Deductions, etc.* Particularly note that Schedule K addresses: *Shareholders' Shares* (PLURAL), whereas Schedule K-1 addresses: *Shareholder's Share* (SINGULAR).

Schedule L	BALANCE SHEETS PER BOOKS		
Assets • Beginning / end of tax year		**C Corp**	**S Corp**
1	Cash on hand		
2	Accounts receivable		
3	Inventories		
4	U.S. Government obligations		
5	Tax exempt securities		
6	Other current assets		
7	Loans to stockholders		
8	Mortgage & real estate loans		
9	Other investments		
10	a. Buildings & other appreciable assets		
	b. Less accumulated depletion	< >	< >
11	a. Depletable assets		
	b. Less accumulated depletion	< >	< >
12	Land (net of any amortization)		
13	a. Intangible assets (amortizable only)		
	b. Less accumulated amortization	< >	< >
14	Other assets		
15	**TOTAL Assets** ////////		
Liabilities & Stockholders' Equity		**C Corp**	**S Corp**
16	Accounts payable		
17	Mortgages, notes, bonds payable (less than 1 yr)		
18	Other current liabilities		
19	Loans from stockholders		
20	Mortgages, notes, bonds payable (1 yr or more)		
21	Other liabilities		
22	Capital stock a. preferred		////////
	b. common		
23	Additional paid-in capital		
24	Retained earnings - Appropriated		////////
25	Retained earnings - Unappropriated		
26	Adjustments to stockholders' equity		
27	Less cost of treasury stock	< >	< >
28	**TOTAL Liabilities & Stockholders' Equity**		

Fig. 3.6 - Items Comprising a "Balance Sheet" on Tax Forms 1120/1120S

Schedule L: Balance Sheets

Alphabetically, the next schedule that appears on Form 1120 *and* Form 1120S is Schedule L. Its official title is: ***Balance Sheets per Books***. Note the two plurals: Sheets and Books. There are two balance sheets: one for the beginning of the year and one for the end of the year. The term "books" refers to books of account. The term refers to all accounting records that the corporation uses for posting and tracking its financial well being. Without going into descriptive detail, we list in Figure 3.6 all of the items that appear on an official Schedule L.

Schedule L is an invaluable resource for determining how efficiently a corporation is run. With it, you can figure its debt-to-equity ratio, its liquidity (cash pus convertibles to cash), and the self-dealings between shareholders and the corporation in the form of loans TO shareholders and loans FROM shareholders. For these and other matters ascertainable from Schedule L, Form 1120 (for C corporations) uses the term *stock*holder, whereas Form 1120S (for S corporations) uses the term *share*holder. Both terms describe the owners of the corporation.

With the exception of two items, the items shown in Figure 3.6 are identical for C and S corporations. The two exceptions are preferred stock (item 22a) and appropriated retained earnings (item 24) which do not apply to S corporations. We think you should take a moment and actually read down the items listed in Figure 3.6. Unless you are, or have been, a managing officer of a corporation, you may not have seen Schedule L before. It is not one of those statements that is routinely furnished to stockholders/shareholders each year.

Ordinarily, the only tax information given to stockholders/shareholders each year is Form 1099-DIV for C corporation dividends, and Schedule K-1 for S corporation distributive share items. Rarely are these "information returns" accompanied by Schedule L. Yet, for small and closely held corporations, there is no valid reason why a Schedule L cannot be provided upon request.

4

COMPENSATION OF OFFICERS

> The Salary Policy In Close Corporations Tends To Be Such That The Officers "Want It All" When Business Is Good, And "Want Protection" When Business Is Bad. To Be Deductible Against Corporate Income, All Salaries Must Be REASONABLE In Light Of Personal Services ACTUALLY RENDERED. At Least 5 Or More Pertinent Factors Must Be Weighed. Though No One Factor Is Determinative, INDICATORS Of Excessive Compensation Are: (1) Absence Of Dividends, (2) Minimal Profits, (3) Rarity Of Retained Earnings, (4) Low Return On Equity, and (5) Unexplained Year End Bonuses.

On page 1 of Forms 1120 and 1120S, the very first deduction line is captioned: *Compensation of officers.* The Form 1120 requires particularly that the five highest paid officers of a C corporation be identified in detail with respect to:

(a) Name of officer,
(b) Social security number,
(c) Percent of time devoted to business,
(d) Percent of common stock ownership,
(e) Percent of preferred stock ownership, and
(f) Amount of compensation.

A separate Schedule E (on page 2 of Form 1120) is designated for this purpose.

There is no corresponding Schedule E on Form 1120S for S corporation officers. Does this mean that the officers of an S corporation do not come under the same compensation and ownership scrutiny as a C corporation? Answer: Of course not. Each S corporation officer is IRS scrutinized via Schedule K-1 (Form 1120S) issued to that person. (Recall Figure 3.5.) There is no corresponding Schedule K-1 for C corporation officers.

What the IRS is looking for is: Do five or fewer officers own 50% or more of the stock of a C or S corporation? If they do, they become the *controlling interests* thereof. This presents opportunities for these few individuals to "adjust" the books and affairs of the corporation to serve primarily their own personal ends. Personal aggrandizement under the guise of allowable deductions for a closely held corporation inherently invites close scrutiny by the IRS. The first target of scrutiny is the amount and reasonableness of compensation paid to the controlling officers.

In this chapter, therefore, we want to address what the tax law says about the deductibility of officer compensation, what the IRS includes in the term, what are the various factors that go into establishing the reasonableness of compensation, the role of time and ownership in the business, instructional court cases thereon, and what happens when a corporation is disallowed a deduction for all or a portion of an officer's compensation. It is often a shock to the owners of small private corporations when they learn of the extent to which the IRS has authority over the amount of compensation paid. Said authority is well grounded in Section 162 of the Internal Revenue Code. Over 800 pages of tax law, Treasury regulations, revenue rulings, and court decisions are on the IRS's side.

Business Necessity Essential

The first hurdle for deductibility of compensation to an officer is that the amount paid must be a bona fide business expense. The expense must be incurred as a necessity for the profit-seeking goals of the corporation. Furthermore, some actual personal service by the officer must be rendered. The fact that the officer may be part owner of the business is not the point. The nature of his service, its relative importance to success of the business, and the kind of hours devoted, dictate the amount of compensation that is deductible. In the strictest sense, the term "compensation" bears no relationship whatever to the percent of ownership of the business the recipient of compensation may have. As a matter of IRS practice, the amount and reasonableness of compensation is determined independently of ownership interests.

The fundamental tax law on point is Section 162: *Trade or Business Expenses*. The compensation of officers is just one — though the foremost one — of multiple deductible expenses. As to compensation paid, the general rule of subsection 162(a)(1) reads:

There shall be allowed as a deduction all the ordinary and necessary expenses paid or incurred during the taxable year in carrying on any trade or business, including—

(1) a reasonable allowance for salaries or other compensation for personal services actually rendered . . .

From these 40 or so statutory words, five criteria emerge for ascertaining the deductibility of officer compensation. To be deductible against the income of a corporation, the compensation **must be—**

1. *ordinary and necessary* to the operation of the business;
2. paid or incurred *in carrying on* the trade or business;
3. allocable to a *specific taxable year*;
4. *reasonable in amount*; and
5. identifiable with personal services *actually rendered.*

For example, suppose a particular officer owns 30% of the stock of a C or S corporation. He is the single-most highest percentage owner. As such, he is given an honorary title of "Assistant Vice President for Operations" and is assigned no expressly specific duties to perform. He shows up on the business premises two to three hours a month and attends regularly all Board of Directors' meetings. He is paid $250,000 a year for his services.

Would such compensation be deductible by the corporation?

Most definitely not. Whatever such officer does, he performs no vital role to the success of the business. His actual performance time is insignificant. In all likelihood, the IRS would disallow his compensation as a deduction to the corporation, and would add it back to its bottom line as earnings and profits. The irony of a situation like this is that, while the corporation gets no deduction, the honorary officer has to pay income tax on the amount he received.

So important are the above basic principles that we present a depiction of them in Figure 4.1. We urge that you study carefully — and possibly memorize — the points in Figure 4.1. They are tax fundamentals that you should be aware of, should you be, or expect to be, an officer of a corporation (whether small or large). Later, we'll cite portions of Treasury Regulation § 1.162-7: *Compensation for personal services.*

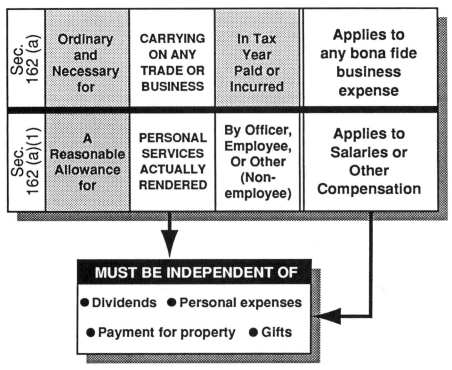

Fig. 4.1 - Tax Law Fundamentals for Deductibility of Officer Compensation

Active Business Requirement

Expressing Figure 4.1 in another way, the deductibility for compensation paid to officers must relate directly to the *carrying on* of a for-profit trade or business. That is, the compensation must not relate to a particular investment, must not be a disguise for personal liability such as payment of alimony, must not be for some hobby or side business venture, must not be in connection with a tax sheltering activity, and must not be a substitute for the sale or exchange of property (whether tangible, real, or intangible). The compensation must relate to an active ongoing business where the personal services performed are essential to the business goodwill and productivity.

There is no statutory definition of the term "trade or business." This is because such term has its origin way back in the early colonial days of this country (circa the 1700s) when customs duties and local taxes were imposed. As used today, the term is generally associated with an activity carried on *with regularity* for economic profit or for livelihood. Furthermore, the compensation paid or incurred must be as remuneration for *active participation* by an officer in the trade or business being carried on.

Similarly, the term "ordinary and necessary" has been recognized over the years as an associative test of the regularity of a business. The term "ordinary" refers to an expenditure that is common and acceptable in the type of business being carried on. If an officer is a financial and investment whiz, for example, and is assigned as a production manager in a business manufacturing kitchen cabinets, his compensation should be based on his talents as a production chief: not as a financial genius. It is just not common practice in a consumer market business to assign an MBA in Finance to the design and manufacture of kitchen products.

The term "necessary" is the knife edge for distinguishing a business expense from a personal expense. It should be self-evident that paying a corporate officer for items purchased for his home, for his family vacations, and for recreational equipment for his children is not a bona fide business expense. Yet, controlling interests in small corporations try to get their company to pay for as many personal items as they can. They do so on the assumption that the corporation can write these matters off as some form of business expense, if not as compensation.

Time and again, the courts have determined that "necessary" means that which is *appropriate and helpful* to the continuation of a business. A good tax case on this point is *Fairmont Homes, Inc.* (45 TCM 1340, Dec. 40,042(M), TC Memo (1983-209). A disgruntled 50% owner of the corporation threatened a lawsuit to close down the company if he did not get his way on salary and policy matters. To induce him to refrain from instigating legal action and from interfering with management decisions, he was paid a handsome salary of nearly $350,000 . . . for staying out of the way. The IRS disallowed this item as a deduction by the corporation. Nevertheless, the U.S. Tax Court ruled that the amount as compensation was necessary in order to avoid jeopardizing the business and its reputation.

What is a "Reasonable" Salary?

In the Fairmont Homes case, the IRS took the position that the salary paid was unreasonable, when measured against actual services performed. It recited Section 162(a)(1) with regard to—

a reasonable allowance for salaries or other compensation for personal services actually rendered.

As evidenced by the Fairmont Homes case, the reasonableness aspect of officer compensation is one of the most frequently contested issues between the IRS and the managers of small C and S corporations. The fact is: There is no legal standard of reasonableness. The nearest such standard is that the compensation not be lavish, extravagant, or excessive. Much, of course, depends on the facts and circumstances of each particular situation. Do keep in mind, though, that our focus is on small, privately held corporations. Quite different rules apply to officer compensation in publicly held corporations.

For salary dollar amounts, there is a practical upper limit. It is $1,000,000 for officers of publicly held corporations. This is so stated in Section 162(m): ***Certain Excessive Employee Remuneration.*** Its general rule in paragraph (1) reads—

In the case of any publicly held corporation, no deduction shall be allowed . . . to the extent that the amount of such remuneration for the taxable year with respect to any covered employee exceeds $1,000,000.

We interpret Section 162(m)(1) for small private corporations as meaning that any salary approaching $1,000,000 per year as *deemed excessive*. Would you not agree?

Treasury Regulation § 1.162-7(b)(1) attempts to clarify the term "excessive" by saying—

*An **ostensible salary** paid by a corporation may be a distribution of dividends on stock. This is likely to occur in the case of a corporation having few shareholders, practically all of whom draw salaries. If in such a case the salaries are in excess of those ordinarily paid for similar services and the excessive payments **correspond or bear a close relationship to the stockholdings of the officers or employees,** it would seem likely that the salaries are not paid wholly for services rendered, but that the excessive payments are a distribution of earnings upon the stock. An ostensible salary may* [also] *be in part payment for property* [tangible, real, or intangible transferred to the corporation by the remunerated person]. [Emphasis added.]

In other words, the IRS takes the position that if there is any "close relationship" to the stockholdings of an officer or of any property transfers by an officer, it deems that salary to be *ostensible*. It then concludes that the salary may consist of:

1. true salary,
2. share of earnings, and/or
3. transfer of property.

Each of these items is tax treated differently. Only the true salary portion is deductible as compensation.

As to the proper amount of compensation deductible, Regulation § 1.162-7(b)(3) says—

*In any event, the allowance for the compensation paid may not exceed what is reasonable under all the circumstances. It is, in general, just to assume that reasonable and true compensation is only such amount as would ordinarily be paid for **like services** by **like enterprises** under **like circumstances**. The circumstances to be taken into consideration are those existing at the date when the contract for services was made, not those existing at the date when the contract is questioned.*

It is regulatory wording like that above that creates so much controversy among successful small business corporations.

General Factors for Decisions

How do the IRS and the courts determine what is reasonable compensation and what is not? What facts and factors do they home in on? The short answer is: Each case is decided on its own facts!

The most frequently cited authority defining reasonable compensation is an early Supreme Court case: *Botany Worsted Mills* (1 USTC ¶ 348, 287 U.S. 282). In that case, the Court determined that—

Extraordinary, unusual and extravagant amounts paid by a corporation to its officers in the guise and form of compensation for their services, but having no substantial relation to the measure of the services, and being utterly disproportionate to their value, are not in reality payment for services and cannot be regarded as "ordinary and necessary" [business] expenses [of the corporation].

Though the above is a scholarly statement of judicatory reasoning, it does not present any concrete factual guidance. Other court decisions — many others — have to be reviewed, in order to extract those factors most pertinent to the decision rendered. It is significant to point out that *no one factor* is judicially conclusive on its own. Several basic factors must be considered by the courts before a meaningful decision can be rendered.

Among the factors commonly considered by the IRS and the courts are:

1. The officer's qualifications and role in the company.
2. Evidence of salaries paid for similar services by comparable businesses.
3. The size, nature, and complexity of the business, and the type of customers served.
4. A comparison of salaries paid to gross sales, net profits, and capital investment.
5. A comparison of salaries with dividends and other distributions to stockholders.
6. The salary policy as to all employees, not just the officers.
7. The amount of compensation paid to the same officers in previous years.
8. Whether the compensation is established at a level, formula, or bonus to absorb most or all of the corporate income.
9. The history of dividend payments as compared to what an independent investor (who is not an officer) might expect from similar businesses.
10. The extent of makeup and correction for prior under-compensation during the early years of the corporation.
11. Any patents, copyrights, or special processes that the officer may have created for the corporation.
12. The extent of obvious personal liabilities, such as the payment of alimony and property settlement for an officer whose marriage has ended or is ending.

Each case stands upon its own facts, and each tax year stands upon the facts existing in that year. Findings made on the question of reasonableness of salaries in one year do not make *res judicata* (already decided) the question of reasonableness in a subsequent year. The issue of "reasonableness" hinges on the expectations of an independent investor. A graphic summary of the above is presented in Figure 4.2.

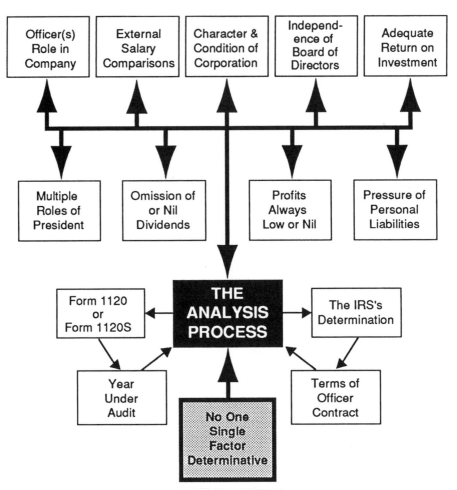

Fig. 4.2 - Factors Considered for Reasonableness of Compensation

Special Factors for Scrutiny

In closely held corporations certain other factors than those above are scrutinized by the IRS before a tax dispute reaches court. This scrutiny focuses most forcefully on the compensation to stockholder-officers where full allowance would leave only a nominal or nil earnings for passing through to nonofficer and nonemployer investors. If this pattern shows up over a period of five to ten years of operation, the IRS bears down hard. The factors which it weighs for extent of allowability of the salaries paid are covered in the following paragraphs.

Board of directors not independent. In the vast majority of close corporations, the founder and principal shareholder, and one or two family members or close business associates, constitute the Board of Directors. As a consequence, little IRS weight is given to any resolution authorizing a compensation amount or formula. Such a "board" cannot be truly independent in its judgment of reasonableness. Whatever the board approves is regarded by the IRS as rubber stamping the principal shareholder's alter ego.

Omission of dividends. The omission of dividends year after year is a telltale sign that the ranking officers "want it all." A for-profit corporation operates on the premise that dividends will be declared each year that the enterprise is profitable. If no dividends are paid when salaries increase noticeably at the end of each year, why is the business holding itself out as a corporation? The entity could just as well be a proprietorship or partnership. Still, there could be valid reasons for no dividends. Sustained losses, extensive borrowings, tax penalties, litigation in process or pending, salaries being below normal when compared with similar businesses, and plain old-fashioned mismanagement can explain the absence of dividends. Our point is that some credible explanation is in order when there is a clear pattern of no dividends.

Fixed salaries plus commissions. In many small businesses, the officers are both managers and sales persons. The practice is to pay a fixed salary plus a commission on gross sales. If such is the case, the fixed portion should be nominal (adjusted only for cost of living increases) and insufficient to support a high lifestyle. The commission portion should be representative of the industry: 5%, 7%, 9%, 11% . . . or whatever. Some system for tracking the sales of each individual officer should be in place. The commission policy and procedures should be on a par with that paid to independent salespersons selling similar products or services outside of the corporation.

Multiple duties of officers. In those corporations where the founder or other originator is talented, innovative, and administrative, he may wear "several hats" simultaneously. He may, for example, be the president, chief technical head, chief financial officer, and general operations manager As such, each corporate title is cordoned off and evaluated as a single-duty assignment. A job description for each assignment is prepared, then compared with what the officer actually does in that post. The hours devoted to each assignment within a regular pay period should be documented. It is not uncommon for multi-duty officers to devote 60^+ hours a week (260^+ hours a month) to the interests of their corporation. Such devotion is an important factor in establishing the reasonableness of his compensation.

Percentage compensation fixed over time. A long-standing plan for percentage compensation (based on a designated accounting reference) is often recognized by the courts, if not always by the IRS, as a reasonable measure of the compensation paid. To be tax accepted, the plan should be adopted early in the corporation's formation and consistently maintained over the years. The plan is viewed very favorably if, in lean years, it works against the officer and for the corporation. In ordinary years, the plan should appear as paying a salary comparable to what the IRS would judge as allowable. In good years, the plan should appear as paying a base salary plus a performance-related bonus. The gross sales of the corporation are a convenient percentage reference, though other statistical references can be used.

The "Dexsil" Appeals Case

It is always instructive to review the judicial rationale that takes place on the issue of reasonableness of officer compensation. One such comparatively recent case is that of the *Dexsil Corp.* (CA-2, 98-1 USTC ¶ 50,471). This case was heard in June 1998 by the US. Court of Appeals for the 2nd Circuit (New York). It was an appeal from a decision of the U.S. Tax Court which, in itself, was an appeal from the IRS ruling. The tax years at issue were 1989 and 1990.

In 1989, the President of Dexsil Corporation (who was also the CEO, Treasurer, and CFO) was paid a salary of $376,500 under a percentage-of-gross-sales compensation plan. In 1990, he was paid $488,000. Both the IRS and the Tax Court considered these amounts to be excessive and unreasonable.

The President had been with the company since its founding in 1977. At that time, there were just three employees including himself; the gross sales then were $53,000. In 1990, the company had 31 employees (including himself); the gross sales in that year were, by comparison, a whopping $4,900,000. Over the entire 14-year period (1977 through 1990), the President's compensation averaged about 11% of gross sales. Up through 1983, his average salary varied between $10,000 and $12,000 per year. In 1984, the company was recapitalized and four new products (on-site detection kits for hazardous contaminants) were designed, developed, and marketed. These new products were the technical and marketing brainchild of the President himself. During 1984 through 1990, the President devoted 60 to 65 hours per week to the Dexsil's business.

For the two years at issue by the IRS, the following accounting statistics were presented to the IRS, to the Tax Court, and to the Appeals Court:

	1989	1990
Gross sales	$3,420,000	$4,900,000
Return on equity	26.3%	25.5%
Retained earnings	$1,670,000	$2,168,000
Dividends paid	$ 16,000	$ 26,000
President's salary	**$ 376,000**	**$ 488,000**
% of gross sales	11%	10%

The IRS allowed $200,000 and disallowed $176,000 for 1989; it then assessed a deficiency tax of $82,700. It allowed $220,000 and disallowed $268,000 for 1990, and further assessed a deficiency tax of $174,200. Upon petition to the U.S. Tax Court, the Court allowed $300,000 for 1989 and reduced the deficiency tax to $33,500. The Court allowed $320,000 for 1990 and reduced the deficiency tax to $95,800. This Tax Court decision was appealed.

The Appellate Court applied four "tests" as to the reasonableness of the compensation paid to the Dexsil President. These tests were:

a. *Relevant Factors* — (1) the president's position, hours worked, duties performed, and innovations made; (2) salary comparisons with similar companies; (3) character and financial condition of the company; and (4) ability to "disguise" dividends as salary.

b. *Expectations of an independent investor* — (1) company's return on equity; (2) the extent to which dividends are paid; (3) capital appreciation of company's stock; and (4) existence of independent investors.

c. *Contingent compensation formula* — (1) when first established; (2) consistently applied through ups and downs of the business; (3) overcompensation in good years, undercompensation in bad years; and (4) adopted in good faith as an incentive agreement.

d *Multiple roles separately compared* — (1) not limited to comparisons of CEOs only; (2) when separate roles of president, treasurer, and CFO are performed, three combined salaries should be considered.

The Appellate Court concluded as follows:

In conclusion, we find the Tax Court's failure to assess the reasonableness of [the Dexsil President's] *compensation . . . erroneous as a matter of law. Accordingly, we vacate and remand . . .* [that] *the Tax Court make specific findings . . . whether, after reconsideration of* [the factors above], *the balance has shifted in favor of Dexsil such that it has met its burden of proving that* [its President's] *compensation was reasonable.*

The "Leonard Pipeline" Case

Here's another instructional Appeals Court case. This time, it is in the 9th Circuit Court of Appeals, San Francisco: *Leonard Pipeline Contractors, Ltd.* (CA-9, 98-1 USTC ¶ 50,356). The Appeals Court reversed and remanded back to the Tax Court that it explain why, after its six years of deliberation (1991-1997), it reached a figure intermediate between what Leonard claimed as compensation for 1987 and what the IRS allowed.

Leonard was a 40-year veteran of the pipeline industry. He formed his own company in 1977 and retired in 1987. At that time, after consulting with an independent accounting firm, he paid himself a retirement bonus. The accounting firm recommended a bonus of 10% of the current gross revenues. In 1987, the gross revenues were around $16,870,400.

From 1977 through 1987, the business generated a grand total of $123,124,900 in gross income. Leonard was the President, Chief Operating Officer, and CFO. In 1985 and 1986, he took no salary while developing a coating, insulating, and wrapping technique for 325 miles of pipeline in Texas, Arizona, and California. He retired in 1987 with a salary of $97,800 and a bonus of $1,680,000.

In 1990, after auditing his 1987 corporate and personal income tax returns, the IRS allowed the salary figure of $97,800. It cut the bonus to a mere $37,400. This was a paltry 0.22% of the $16,870,400 in gross revenues in 1987. And, of course, whopping deficiency taxes and penalties were assessed. The dispute went to Tax Court in 1991. The Tax Court's decision was not rendered until 1997 — a full six years later.

The Tax Court judge concluded that—

Any attempt to determine reasonable compensation with mathematical precision is impossible. . . . Using our best judgment, we conclude that $700,000 would represent a reasonable amount of compensation: $400,000 for salary and bonus, and $300,000 as a lump sum retirement payment.

The Appellate Court reversed the Tax Court and remanded that it spell out a better reasoning for its decision. The Appellate Court particularly wanted an explanation why a bonus for past inadequately-compensated services was given a "neutral" factor, when no prior bonus had ever been paid. The Appellate Court also pointed out that the return on investment in 1987 would have satisfied an independent investor and that, as a result, Leonard "had a right" to increased compensation.

Treatment of Excess Compensation

What happens if, after all of the appeals and reviews, an amount of compensation is deemed excessive? Suppose, for example, in the Leonard Pipeline case above, the Tax Court, upon reconsideration decided that a retirement bonus of $1,000,000 was reasonable. How is the excess amount of $680,000 tax treated by Leonard **and** by his corporation?

Answer: Two different ways.

With respect to Leonard as an individual, he pays full income tax on it. Because he received the money, he pays tax on it on the premise that it is "in lieu" compensation. It is treated as in lieu of dividends, in lieu of payment for property, or in lieu of a gift from the company. No matter what the IRS characterizes such excess as, it is still taxable money to the recipient.

With respect to Leonard Pipeline as a corporation, the disallowed compensation becomes a **lost deduction**. It cannot be deducted as compensation of officers. Therefore, it is added back to the net earnings of the business. As a C corporation, the addback would be taxed and penalized to the corporation. As an S corporation, it would be passed through to all shareholders other than Leonard himself (he has already paid tax on it). Each of said shareholders would pay tax and penalty in proportion to his ownership interests. This is a way of tax punishing the minority shareholders for their failure to voice limitations on what the company's bonus policy should be.

The deduction lost to the corporation can be mitigated (somewhat) by a written agreement requiring that any excess compensation to officers be paid back. To be allowed by the IRS, however, the payback agreement must be included in the corporation bylaws, after having been proposed, discussed, and adopted by its Board of Directors. It should apply to all employees and to all shareholders, and not just to a single officer-shareholder. Otherwise, the IRS will regard any on-the-spot payback arrangement as evidence that the corporation was well aware that its officer-compensation policy was excessive.

5

WHEN UNDERCAPITALIZED

The Purpose Of Doing Business In Corporate Form Is To Provide An Adequate Capital Pool To Meet Ordinary Operating Needs Year After Year. The Providers Of This "Money Pool" Are The Stockholders. When Chronically Under-capitalized, The IRS Gets Concerned, Especially When Trust Fund Taxes (EmployEE WITHHOLDINGS And EmployER MATCHINGS) Are Delinquent. It Then Takes A Hard Look At Officer Salaries, Employee Benefits, "Loans" From Stockholders, And Why The Special Rule Of Section 1244 Is Not Used. In Event Of Petition For Bankruptcy, The IRS Can Immediately Assess All PRIOR UNPAID Taxes.

How many times have you heard some small-business owner say: "We have a cash flow problem this month." Or, "We are cash short and have to extend our line of credit." Or, maybe you have made these or similar statements yourself.

Being cash short is a perennial problem with small corporations, the entrepreneurial owners of which have big ideas. They substitute creativity at using other people's money for inadequate capitalization of their own. The most common reason given for being cash starved is that: "The Government (meaning the IRS and state agencies) has taken all of our cash for payroll taxes, tax withholdings, and sales taxes (where applicable)." Perhaps they have. But these matters can be foreseen. And so can many other transactional matters in running a business be foreseen.

The position taken by tax and regulatory agencies is that when conducting business in corporate form, the owners should anticipate and provide for the operational cash needs of the enterprise. This is what business planning and management are supposed to be all about To the IRS, perennial undercapitalization is an indicator of planned bankruptcy. The telltale signs include heavy debt load, high officer salaries, lavish travel and entertainment, and exotic expansion plans designed to lure in more of other people's money. The IRS is always concerned about potential bankruptcy when under-capitalization takes center stage. It does not want to be left with delinquent taxes that someday may be uncollectible.

In this chapter, therefore, we want to discuss the "indicators" of undercapitalization as viewed by the IRS, what you are expected to do to prevent such likelihood, and the various tax laws — such as Section 1244, for example — that can be used against you . . . or for you. We also want to tell you about the treatment of below-market-rate loans (from family members), the 100% penalty on payroll withholdings, and the *immediate assessment authority* of the IRS, should you file for bankruptcy. As a corporation, all financial matters have to be accounted for, to the very end.

What is Expected of You

When you form a corporation, or after it is formed and operating and you become an officer thereof, there are certain expectations of you. You are expected to assure that the entity is adequately capitalized to pursue its business goals. After all, the idea behind a corporation is that there is a stockholder capital pool out there which can be tapped for entrepreneurial risks. Being under-capitalized means that the stockholders are not bearing their expected burden of risks. Lenders — as opposed to stockholders — are not supposed to bear the risks. This is because lenders do not share in the profits and losses of the business, as shareholders do.

The "capitalization" of a corporation is that which is represented by its capital stock, current profits, and retained earnings (prior years' profits which have not been distributed to the stockholders). Thus, capitalization is the *total investment* in the business by the owners thereof. Said investment must be adequate to at least meet the current liabilities of the business. Except for thefts, casualties, and natural disasters, most current liabilities can be foreseen.

To illustrate the adequacy or inadequacy of capitalization, let us assume the following example. Five business associates put up a total of $150,000 of their own money to form and operate a corporation. All five are salaried employees thereof. During one of the operating years, the owners are able to borrow $350,000 from a commercial lender. The loan is to be amortized over five years at 8% per annum interest. The current year's gross income is $565,000. The corresponding operating expenses are $550,000. These expenses include $200,000 in salaries to the five owner/employees; $20,000 in payroll taxes (excluding employees' money withheld); $25,000 in interest paid on the loan; $47,000 in fixed expenses (rent, insurance, utilities, etc.); $193,000 for cost of goods sold; and $65,000 in other expenses (depreciation, advertising, shipping, office expenses, etc.). The net profit for the year is $15,000 [565,000 – 550,000]. Is this business undercapitalized, overcapitalized, or just right? Be aware that the debt service on this business is $70,000 per year ($350,000 loan amortized over five years). Debt service (repayment of principal) is not a tax allowable operating expense.

The answer to the question is: The business is **under**capitalized.

The first indicator is the salaries paid to the owner employees. The five owner/employees put up $150,000 . . . yet they paid themselves $200,000. The net effect is that they paid $50,000 of their salaries out of borrowed money. This is always a danger signal for any corporation.

The owners' total investment in the business is $165,000 ($150,000 capital stock plus $15,000 current year's profit).

Correspondingly, if the owners cut their salaries to zero (which they can do), the total current-year liability of the business is $420,000. This figure derives from the $550,000 operating expenses above, *less* the $200,000 in salaries, *plus* $70,000 repayment of one year's principal on the $350,000 loan.

The net result is that the business is current-year undercapitalized by $255,000 ($420,000 liability minus $165,000 investment). Thus, for the year illustrated, the owners (initial stockholders) should have put up approximately $400,000 of their own money (250,000 + 150,000) instead of only $150,000.

Stockholder Reluctance

Operating a business undercapitalized year after year is the sure road to bankruptcy. When the stockholders are asked to contribute additional capital to meet their entrepreneurial liabilities, the typical reaction is:

> Not me. If the company is facing insolvency, I don't want to throw good money after bad. Why doesn't the corporation borrow the needed money from commercial lenders? Let them take the risks. I've put up all that I care to risk.

All commercial lenders have their own criterion of qualifying financial statistics before lending to a small private corporation. As a general rule, unless the net worth of the corporation (total assets minus total liabilities) is *twice* that of the amount of loan being sought, the loan application will be disapproved. Every commercial lender wants to see some "equity cushion" in the business before lending to the corporation direct. This is the nature of any lending business. An undercapitalized corporation is not the type of customer commercial lenders want.

In some cases, applying to venture capitalists may work. Such venturers are not too concerned about the current net worth of a corporation seeking money. Their focus is on the proprietary interests (patents, copyrights, trademarks, formulas, niche markets, Internet prospects, etc.) that the private corporation may have. Venture capitalists are more willing if there are prospects of the corporation going public one day. Said capitalists are not easy prey as providers of money. They drive a hard bargain and usually wind up holding the controlling interests in the entity.

There is also the Small Business Administration (SBA). The SBA is a government guarantor of loans provided by commercial banks. The SBA focus is on small struggling businesses which have potential of being sold, and the loan paid off. Unfortunately, the administrative paperwork required for application is overbearing . . . and depressing. The approval process focuses on correcting perceived social and economic injustices for disadvantaged culture groups. For society overall, this is a worthwhile focus. But whether you can count on the SBA or any other government agency as your money guarantor is another matter.

Seeking lenders' money for a small privately-held corporation boils down to one fact. The stockholders themselves have to come up with the money . . . somehow. The most realistic "somehow" is for one or more of the stockholders owning real property (their personal residences, commercial/residential rentals, undeveloped land) to refinance the property and assign the proceeds to the corporation. The corporation is then expected to pay the mortgage principal and interest. In other words, the stockholders are the guarantors of the commercial loan. This can work only if all of the majority stockholders pledge their own properties as security for the loan(s). If only one stockholder is willing to do so, he is shouldering, single-handedly, the risk that should have been shared with other stockholders. This does not make business sense, unless the one stockholder himself owns more than 50% of the voting stock of the corporation.

For an instructional overview of the points above made, and the next point coming up, we present Figure 5.1. The long and short of our message in Figure 5.1 is that, unless your small C or S corporation has miracle-like potential, raising needed capital will fall mostly on those stockholders who are owner-employees.

Below-Market Loans

There is one way to raise needed capital without going through the intense scrutiny of commercial lenders. It is for each stockholder to solicit his/her family and friends. The first approach is to have them buy minority shares in the corporation. This seldom works unless the corporation has some proprietary product or service that could lead to big money later on. Otherwise, family and friends, like the stockholders themselves, tend to be reluctant to add capital to an undercapitalized entity.

In many cases, family and friends would prefer to lend money to persons whom they have known for many years, on that person's personal promise to repay. They would rather take a chance on their

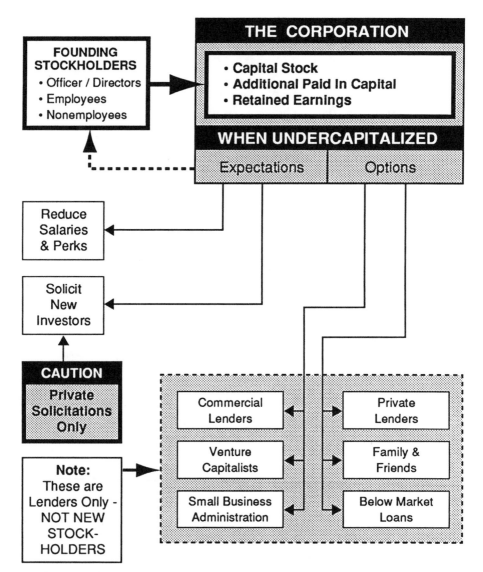

Fig. 5.1 - Expectations & Options When Corporation Undercapitalized

personal relations holding up than on the risk that the corporation might default, leaving them as an unsecured creditor. As a result, money is loaned "between persons" in the form of *Promissory Notes*. This is a highly informal process. The necessary legal forms with appropriate blank spaces can be purchased from office supply stores for modest cost. Because of the personalized nature of the arrangement, interest due on the principal may or may not be stated. If the rate of interest is not stated, or if stated and is below commercial rates, the loans are tax characterized as: *Below-Market Interest Rate* loans.

The tax treatment of below-market loans is addressed in Section 7872: *Treatment of Loans With Below-Market Interest Rates*. This is an 1,800-word tax law. The portion pertinent to us is subsection (c)(1)(C). It is designated: *Corporation-shareholder loans*. Such loan is defined as—

Any below-market loan directly or indirectly between a corporation and any shareholder of such corporation.

In essence, there are three categories of corporation-shareholder below-market loans. These are:

A. Gift loans — not over $10,000 whereby the foregone interest may be forgiven as a gift.

B. Demand loans — not over $100,000 whereby the foregone interest is taxable only to the extent of the investment income generated from the loan.

C. Term loans — over $100,000 whereby the foregone interest is fully taxable at Applicable Federal Rates (AFRs): short-term (less than 3 years), intermediate-term (3 to 9 years), and long-term (over 9 years).

The term "foregone interest" is the amount by which the stated rate of interest agreed upon between the parties is below the corresponding AFR at the time the loan is made. Our point is that Section 7872 recognizes, favorably, below-market loans up to $100,000. The significant requirement is that the amount of capital received by the corporation be entered into its liability ledger as: *Loans from stockholders*. At the same time, the payback terms are to be documented with promissory notes, suitably signaturized.

Section 1244 Stock

On the liabilities side of a balance sheet of a corporation (Schedule L: *Balance Sheets per Books*), the IRS casts a jaundiced eye at the "Loans from stockholders." If the amount shown is more than 50 percent of the stockholders' equity in the corporation, alarm bells can go off. This takes us back to square one. Stockholders are supposed to bear the brunt of all entrepreneurial risks. Why is this risk being diluted with *loans* from stockholders rather than with additional contributions of capital from stockholders?

The usual stockholder response to such a question is:

> Well, if the corporation doesn't make it, I have a capital loss which is tax limited to a $3,000 writeoff per year. On the other hand, if it is a loan loss, I can write off the full amount as an ordinary business loss.

Hold on! This kind of response illustrates the lack of knowledge of Section 1244 . . . otherwise referred to as: *section 1244 stock*. Are you familiar with Section 1244?

It is titled: *Losses on Small Business Stock*. Its general rule is subsection (a) which reads in full—

> *In the case of an individual, a loss on section 1244 stock issued to such individual or to a partnership which would (but for this section) be treated as a loss from the sale or exchange of a capital asset* **shall**, *to the extent provided in this section,* **be** *treated as an ordinary loss*. [Emphasis added.]

The clause "to the extent provided in this section" refers primarily to subsection (b): *Maximum Amount for Any Taxable Year*. The maximum ordinary loss writeoff is $50,000 per year (or $100,000 in the case of husband and wife filing a joint return). This compares most favorably with the $3,000 per year maximum writeoff of a net capital loss. Any unused ordinary loss from 1244 stock in excess of $50,000/$100,000 (for a given year) is treated as a capital loss. The excess net capital loss over $3,000 can be carried over and used in subsequent years.

Subsection (c)(1) defines section 1244 stock as—

stock in a domestic corporation if—
(A) at the time such stock is issued, such corporation was a small business corporation,
(B) such stock was issued . . . for money or other property . . ., and
(C) such corporation, during the period of its 5 most recent taxable years . . ., derived more than 50 percent of its aggregate gross receipts from [active trade or business] *sources. . . .*

For purposes of Section 1244 only, a "small business corporation" is defined as such **if**—

*the aggregate amount of money or other property received by the corporation for stock, as a contribution to capital, and as paid-in surplus **does not exceed $1,000,000*** [subsec. (c)(3)(A)]. [Emphasis added.]

Hence, the IRS has little patience for operating a small C or S corporation undercapitalized when its issued stock aggregates less than $1,000,000.   This is because Section 1244 was much liberalized in 1978. Except for de minimis amounts (under $10,000 per individual stockholder), the IRS takes a dim view of any "Loans from stockholders" that appear on the balance sheets.

Because of the importance of Section 1244 in avoiding undercapitalization, we list its subsections and paragraphs for you in Figure 5.2. There is much vital information there that you should dig out on your own.

Conditions for 1244 Stock

Being a domestic C or S small business corporation, in and of itself, does not automatically qualify its common stock as Section 1244 stock. More affirmative action than this needs to take place.

First, the Board of Directors of the corporation have to adopt a resolution designating which shares (number of shares, purchase price, and certificate numbers) constitute the Section 1244 stock. For example, the directors may specify that 8,000 shares at a

Internal Revenue Code	Subchapter P: CAPITAL GAINS & LOSSES		
Part IV	Special Rules for Determining Gains & Losses		
Sec. 1244	LOSSES ON SMALL BUSINESS STOCK		

Sub. Sec.	Para.	Caption.	Comments
(a)	-	General Rule	Treated as ordinary loss
(b)	-	Maximum for any Taxable Year	$50,000 single $100,000 joint
(c)	-	Section 1244 Stock Defined	——
-	(1)	In General	Domestic small business corp.
-	(2)	Rules for paragraph (1) (C)	5 most recent years
-	(3)	Small Business Corp. Defined	Capital not over $1,000,000
(d)	-	Special Rules	——
-	(1)	Limitations on Ordinary Loss	Not to exceed property value
-	(2)	Recapitalizations; Changes in Name	As per regulations
-	(3)	Relationship to NOL Deduction	Same as trade or business
-	(4)	Individual Defined	Not a trust or estate
(e)	-	Regulations Prescribed	As may be necessary

Fig. 5.2 - List of Subsections and Paragraphs in Section 1244

purchase price of $125 per share shall be classed as 1244 stock (8,000 sh x $125/sh = $1,000,000). The directors must also specify the certificate numbers. For example, a good system is to prefix the designated shares with the numbers "1244". Thus, the first of the 8,000 shares would be numbered 1244-0001; the last certificate number of the 8,000 shares would be 1244-8000. All shares issued thereafter would be certificate number 8001 . . . and so on.

Concurrent with the above, a separate shareholders register must be set up. This is to record and track the issuance of 1244 stock.

Such records are required by Regulation § 1.1244(e)–1(a). The record must show—

(i)   to whom the 1244 stock was issued,

(ii)   the date of issuance to each stockholder,

(iii)   the amount of *money* paid as consideration,

(iv)   the fair market value of *property* paid as consideration, and

(v)   at the time of issuance of each 1244 share, the percentage of gross receipts represented by ordinary trade or business activities, as opposed to passive activities (such as rents, royalties, dividends, interest, and sales or exchanges of securities).

As indicated at items (iii) and (iv) above, 1244 stock can only be issued when money and/or property is paid for such stock. No other form of consideration qualifies. However, other forms of consideration can be accepted for non-1244 stock. This means that there can be two forms of common stock: 1244 and non-1244. When this happens, there may occur what is called: the *transition year*. This is the first taxable year in which the total capital stock (1244 plus non-1244) exceeds $1,000,000.

When the transition occurs, Regulation § 1.1244(c)–2(b)(2): *Requirement of designation in event $1,000,000 limitation exceeded*, comes into play. The essence of this regulation is that the designation of 1244 stock must be reconfirmed (by the directors) for the transition year and thereafter. The reconfirmation must be done—

no later than the 15th day of the third month following the close of the transitional year.

An instructional digest of the above is presented in Figure 5.3.

If no reconfirmation is made when required, the unissued 1244 stock loses its prima facie ordinary loss treatment of Section 1244. A limited portion of the Section 1244 treatment can be recouped, however, under the procedures of paragraph (3) of the above regulation. These procedures require that all issued 1244 stock, plus all additions to capital, plus all paid-in surplus capital, before the

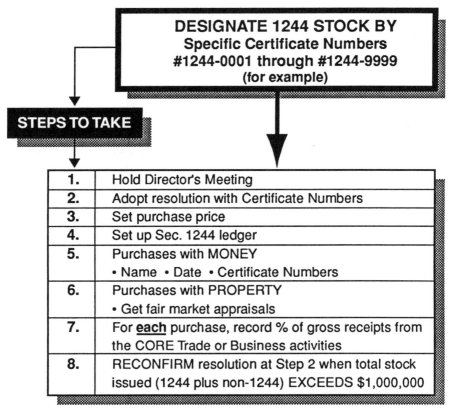

DESIGNATE 1244 STOCK BY
Specific Certificate Numbers
#1244-0001 through #1244-9999
(for example)

STEPS TO TAKE

1.	Hold Director's Meeting
2.	Adopt resolution with Certificate Numbers
3.	Set purchase price
4.	Set up Sec. 1244 ledger
5.	Purchases with MONEY • Name • Date • Certificate Numbers
6.	Purchases with PROPERTY • Get fair market appraisals
7.	For **each** purchase, record % of gross receipts from the CORE Trade or Business activities
8.	RECONFIRM resolution at Step 2 when total stock issued (1244 plus non-1244) EXCEEDS $1,000,000

Fig. 5.3 - Specific Requirements for Qualifying Small Business Stock

transition date, be *subtracted* from $1,000,000. The residual amount is then allocated to the 1244 stock buyers in proportion to the total capital received, after the transition date.

For example, suppose there is $200,000 of unissued 1244 stock available for sale after the transition date. No redesignation/ reconfirmation was made. The total after-transition capital stock issued (1244 and non-1244) comes to $500,000 (for example). The "qualified" portion of the 1244 stock eligible for Section 1244 redesignation treatment is limited to—

$$\frac{200,000}{500,000} \times \$200,000 = 0.40 \times \$200,000 = \$80,000$$

For this example, $120,000 (200,000 − 80,000) in Section 1244 benefits is lost entirely. It cannot be recouped. The unissued 1244 stock automatically becomes non-1244 stock. Any losses thereafter on its sale or exchange become capital losses.

Payroll Withholdings & Taxes

For undercapitalized businesses, the most chronic cash flow problem has to do with payroll withholdings and payroll taxes. The problems are chronic because the withholdings and taxes have to be collected and paid over to the IRS (and to state employment taxing agencies) on a monthly basis. This means that as long as the corporation has one employee or more, the payovers have to be made month after month . . . ad infinitum. This chronic burden is common knowledge for any business that has employees, from the president of the company on down.

Payroll withholdings (employee money) and payroll taxes (employer money) are two different — though coordinated — accounting activities. The withholdings from employees comprise such items as—

(1)	federal income tax	}	
(2)	one-half of social security tax	}	
(3)	one-half of medicare tax	}	EMPLOYEE
(4)	state income tax	}	MONEY
(5)	state disability tax	}	

Taxes paid by the employer for the privilege of having employees consist of:

(a)	one-half of social security tax	}	
(b)	one-half of medicare tax	}	
(c)	federal unemployment tax	}	EMPLOYER
(d)	state unemployment insurance tax	}	MONEY
(e)	state training tax (as applicable)	}	

The IRS and state agencies provide tables, rules, and instructions for computing the amount of employee withholdings to withhold, and for computing the employer taxes thereon. The withholdings and payroll taxes apply to all wages, salaries, bonuses, commissions, and other forms of remuneration (whether cash or any medium other than cash) for personal services rendered to the corporation. Regardless of the magnitude of the combined employee withholdings and employer taxes, **cash deposits** must be made. Such deposits are required semi-weekly, monthly, or quarterly, as follows:

1. for amounts over $50,000   — semi-weekly deposits (7-day grace period)
2. for amounts not over $50,000   — monthly deposits (15-day grace period)
3. for amounts not over $1,000   — quarterly deposits (30-day grace period)

For illustrative simplicity, let's assume an annual payroll of $500,000. That would be a monthly payroll of about $41,667. From this amount, about 32% (federal) would constitute employee withholdings ($13,333) for income tax and social security/medicare. This would leave a net payroll of $28,334 (41,667 − 13,333). Additionally, about 8% (federal) would constitute employer taxes ($3,334). Altogether then, $45,000 (28,334 net payroll + 13,333 employee withholdings + 3,334 employer tax) is paid out in cash each month. Payments to employees, and the payover of withholdings and employer taxes are top priority of cash outflows. Said payments take priority over those to suppliers, creditors, and contractors.

The 100% Trust Fund Penalty

In the $500,000 annual payroll example above, $16,667 per month (13,333 + 3,334) constitutes what is called: *trust fund money*. For a full year, that's $200,000 (12 x $16,667) of such money. If we add state withholdings and unemployment tax, another $50,000 or so would be involved. Altogether, that's about $250,000 cash just from employees alone. When a corporation is chronically cash short, there is an overwhelming urge to use the

$250,000 to pay suppliers, creditors, and contractors in order to keep the business going. This practice leads to the 100% trust fund penalty.

The term "trust fund" is a legal doctrine for penalty administration purposes. In reality, no actual trust entity exists. The doctrine is based on the legal theory that a transitory trust takes effect, from the moment that withholding is first required, until all required withholdings and taxes are paid over. The actual trust entity is the U.S. Treasury (for federal withholdings) and state treasuries (for state withholdings). Employers are regarded as intermediate trusts — they are on the honor system — from time of collection to time of payover.

For any failure to collect or any failure to pay over, Section 6672 applies. This IR Code section is officially titled: **Failure to Collect and Pay Over Tax, or Attempt to Evade or Defeat Tax**. Note that there are two distinct clauses in this title, namely: *Failure to . . .* and *Attempt to . . . .* Both clauses target those businesses which are cash short and having difficulties making their payover deposits on time. In other words, you cannot use trust fund money for other than trust fund depository purposes. It is **sacred money**! It is so, no matter how financially destitute your corporation may be. It is better to forgo officer salaries and employee perks than to misdirect — even temporarily — the trust fund money.

The seriousness of trust fund treatment is expressed in subsection 6672(a) as follows:

Any person required to collect, truthfully account for, and pay over any tax imposed by [the Internal Revenue Code] *who willfully fails to collect such tax, or truthfully account for, and pay over such tax, or who willfully attempts in any manner to evade or defeat any such tax or the payment thereof, shall, in addition to other penalties provided by law, be liable to a **penalty equal to** the total amount of the tax evaded, or not collected, or not accounted for, and not paid over.*

Do you have any idea what the term "penalty equal to" means? It means that the applicable penalty is 100% of the trust fund money that was not accounted for and not paid over. The date for assessment of the 100% penalty is the due date when the "accounted for" depository amounts were required to be made. For administrative reasons, this is 30 days after the close of each calendar quarter (March, June, September, December).

The "penalty equal to" is **another source** for the collection enforcement of not-paid-over withholdings. It is not a punishment penalty in the ordinary tax delinquency sense. It is a *civil liability* imposed upon some identifiable responsible person.

As depicted in Figure 5.4, the trust fund doctrine gives the IRS a choice. It can collect the withheld tax (or that which was required to be withheld) either from the business entity itself, or from the responsible person or persons in charge of the corporation.

Responsible Person Defined

Note the leadoff wording in Section 6672(a): *Any person required to* . . . . The term "any person" means any *responsible person* who is required to collect, account for, and pay over. The liability target is a **person**, a human being: not the business entity itself. The statutory point is that some human is ultimately responsible — the corporate "shield" notwithstanding.

The trust fund recovery penalty can be assessed against the employing corporation, but is most often levied on at least one "responsible person." Such person is usually that individual within the business entity who had sufficient authority to pay over the withheld taxes. This definition includes that individual who had direct responsibility for collecting, accounting for, and paying over the withheld taxes. Such individual is not easy to identify where businesses in closely-held corporate form "pass the buck" among officers, employees, directors, or shareholders.

When tax withholding matters go awry, many would-be responsible persons point fingers at others. This behavior has led the courts to take a broad view when trying to pinpoint the one person ultimately responsible. This pinpointing includes determining who in the corporation has—

    (1)   authority for the decision not to pay trust fund taxes;
    (2)   effective power to pay the taxes;

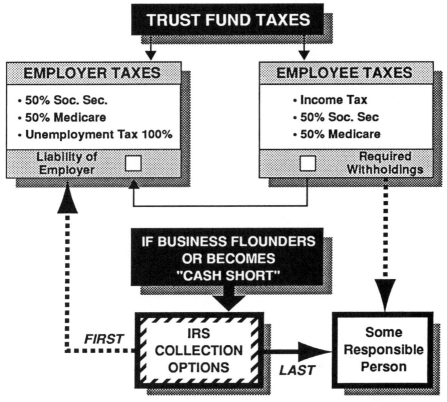

Fig. 5.4 - Civil Liability of the Trust Fund Penalty

(3) authority over the expenditure of funds or the authority to direct payment of creditors;
(4) significant control or authority over the business entity's general finances or general decision-making; or
(5) power to control the decision-making process by which the employer allocates funds.

Thus, a person may be a responsible person for purposes of Section 6672(a), and not even know that withholding taxes have not been paid over. One does not cease to be a responsible person merely by delegating responsibility to someone else. Moreover, Section 6672(a) expressly applies to "any" responsible person: not the person "most" responsible for the tax payovers. There may be

— indeed, there usually are — multiple responsible persons in any business entity engaging employees over a period of years. The IRS, however, can target any **one** of such multiple persons for its assessment and collection of the penalty.

Scrutiny of Employee Benefits

When a corporation is chronically undercapitalized, there is another arena (besides officer compensation and trust fund inattention) that the IRS focuses on. The arena is that of employee benefit plans and programs. Whereas the term "plans" refers to retirement-related benefits (pensions, annuities, life insurance, etc.), the term "programs" refers to accident/health insurance, dependent care assistance, education assistance, and so on. Retirement plans and assistance programs, if not lavish or extravagant, are allowable deductions against the corporation's income.

When a company is cash short, where does the money come from for paying generous employee benefits? Is trust fund money being used? Are creditors being deprived of their payments? Are suppliers being short changed? Are tax payments delinquent? And so on. A prosperous company does not have to address these IRS concerns. It can afford to pay for employee benefits out of its earnings and profits. An undercapitalized entity has to get benefit money from *other than* earnings and profits.

The existence of excessive employee benefits can be determined from four deduction items on Form 1120/1120S. These are:

1. Pension, profit-sharing, etc. *plans*
2. Employee benefit *programs*

3. Compensation of officers
4. Salaries and wages (of other employees)

If we divide the sum of items 1 and 2 (employee benefits) by the sum of items 3 and 4 (employee compensation), we get a benefits-to-compensation (BTC) ratio for the entity.

A BTC ratio of not over 10% is considered frugal. A ratio of 15% to 18% is "about normal" for solvent companies.

If the BTC ratio reaches or exceeds 25%, watch out! Something definitely is amiss. This is especially so, if the interests of stockholders, creditors, and suppliers are being passed over and ignored. At this point, the IRS becomes concerned that it, too, will be passed over.

Immediate Assessment Authority

When a corporation is failing, who knows about the circumstances before all others?

Answer: The corporate officers and majority shareholders. These are the principals who guide and control the business affairs of the entity. But when facing insolvency, receivership, or bankruptcy, they quietly head for the exits.

The typical "heading for the exits" goes like this. The principals seal off their salary packages, bonus arrangements, and retirement contributions by the entity. They engage a high-powered legal firm to prepare themselves against any creditor attack, including the IRS. Through finessing techniques, they assign some innocent lower-level employee to close out the books, if they are closed out at all. The close-out employee is given limited check-writing authority on dwindling entity funds. Such funds have long since been raided by the principals. Either intentionally or unintentionally, they have designated the close-out employee to be the responsible person for IRS target purposes.

Fully 99.9% of all small corporation bankruptcy petitions include tax delinquencies. These delinquencies are of two types: trust fund taxes and nontrust fund taxes. Because federal taxes are essential to the operation of government, the IRS is granted priority in filing its Proof of Claim with the Bankruptcy Court. Such is the essence of IR Code Section 6871: *Claims for Income . . . Taxes in Receivership Proceedings, Etc.*

The general rule is subsection 6871(a): *Immediate Assessment.* It reads in pertinent part—

On the appointment of a receiver for the taxpayer [individual or corporate debtor] *. . . before any court of the U.S. . . ., any deficiency (together with all interest, additional amounts, and* *additions to tax) determined by the* [IRS] *in respect of a tax imposed by subtitle A* [Income Taxes] . . . *on such taxpayer may,* . . . *be immediately assessed if such deficiency* **has not been theretofore assessed** *in accordance with law.*

The emphasized clause: "has not been theretofore assessed," refers to **prepetition dates** of the bankruptcy petition. Once a valid receivership or bankruptcy petition has been filed by a debtor, the Bankruptcy Court has sole jurisdiction over the debtor's estate (including delinquent taxes). Thereafter, all assessment and collection efforts by the IRS and all proceedings before the Tax Court are automatically stayed. A Trustee is appointed by the Bankruptcy Court to prepare a schedule of the priority of claims against the debtor corporation. At the top of this schedule are the trust fund taxes. These taxes are NOT DISCHARGEABLE in bankruptcy.

There is an express exception for trust fund taxes. It appears in Section 6658(b): ***Coordination with*** [Bankruptcy Code], *as—*

Subsection (a) [dischargeability of certain tax liabilities] ***shall not apply*** *to any liability for an addition to the tax which arises from the failure to pay or deposit a tax withheld or collected from others and required to be paid to the United States.*

After the trust fund tax issue is out of the way, the IRS takes its place in line with other secured creditors. It gets a measure of priority, but not absolute priority. Its measure of priority is expressed in Section 6873(a) ***Unpaid Claims***, to wit—

Any portion of a claim for taxes ***allowed*** *in a receivership proceeding which is unpaid shall be paid by the taxpayer* [individual or corporate debtor] *upon* ***notice and demand*** *from the* [IRS] *after the termination of such* [bankruptcy] *proceeding.*

In other words, after adjudication in the Bankruptcy Court, the IRS can still go after the responsible persons of the former corporation. Furthermore, it has **10 years** in which to do so! [Section 6502(a)(1).]

6

METHODS OF ACCOUNTING

Corporations Can Select A Calendar Year, Or A Fiscal Year Where Any 12-Month Period "Frames In" The Natural Business Cycle. Small Corporations Can Select The Cash Method, The Accrual Method, Or A Hybrid (Cash/Accrual) Method For General Books Of Account. The Chosen Method **MUST CLEARLY REFLECT INCOME.** Special Methods Are Prescribed For Capital Gains, Installment Sales, Organizational Costs, Depreciation Allowances, Etc. Inventory Capitalization And End-Of-Year Valuation Methods Can Be Simple Or Complex. If No Consistent Proper Method Is Used, The IRS "Steps In" To So Prescribe.

At the top of Form 1120 or Form 1120S (just below the form title), there is the statement:

For calendar year_____ , or tax year beginning _____,
and ending _____ .

This is your first hint that particular accounting rules must be followed when establishing your corporation's taxable year. This is normally a 12-month period. Though, when first starting or closing out a corporation, a "short" taxable year is permitted. When changing from a C corporation to an S corporation, or when an S corporation automatically lapses into a C, a short taxable year is mandatory. There are times when selecting a corporation's taxable year — especially in a closely held entity — can get confusing.

At the top of page 2 of Form 1120 or Form 1120S, there is Schedule A: *Cost of Goods Sold*. At this schedule you'll see various spaces, checkboxes, and questions that address your method of inventory accounting. If you carry a beginning and ending inventory, as most corporations do, this area alone can become awkward and unwieldy. This is because the IRS always wants to *minimize* your cost of good sold. By doing so, your taxable income is automatically increased.

If you look at Schedule K: *Other Information* on page 3 of Form 1120, or at Schedule B: *Other Information* on page 2 of Form 1120S, you'll see another reference to accounting matters. On both forms you are directed to—

    1. Check method of accounting: (a) ☐ *Cash, (b)* ☐ *Accrual, (c)* ☐ *Other (specify)* ▶ _____.

In this chapter, therefore, we want to review those methods of accounting that affect the preparing and filing of Forms 1120 and 1120S. In the process, we want to point to particular cautions to take to demonstrate *consistency* in accounting techniques. Every change in an accounting year or method, unless expressly provided for in law, requires IRS approval. For a change in year, a 4-page Form 1128 must be filed; for a change in method, an 8-page Form 3115 is required. As a consequence, proper accounting is a big deal when it comes to establishing the taxable income of a corporation. It's an even bigger deal for small corporations where a handful of owners and managers can skew the books and records to achieve the taxable income result that they want.

Selection of Tax Year

It is general knowledge that the accounting period for income taxation is annual. That is, once every 12 consecutive months. The annual ritual of income tax preparation goes on year after year . . . after year. This process is called the "annual theory of taxation." The tax return for a given year must show the net results from all transactions occurring during the year. Every taxpayer knows this.

For individuals, the required accounting period is a calendar year. A calendar years ends — and must end — on December 31. Calendar years are also prescribed for individually focused entities, such as proprietorships, partnerships, and trusts.

For corporations, however, a *fiscal year* accounting period can be used. This is any 12-month period ending on the last day of any month other than December. The tax rationale for a fiscal year is to "frame in" an entire cycle of the ups and downs in the natural flow of a business. The fiscal year goal is to produce an equalizing effect on the business income and deductions throughout the selected 12 months. This is tax essential, even though the predominant income may be generated within six months or less. As you know, the income tax rates do not change from month to month. They are annual tax rates. Thus, the selection of a corporation's fiscal year must be made with the concept in mind of "annualizing" the income and outgo over a 12-month period.

The tax law on point is Section 441: *Period for Computation of Taxable Income.* Extracts pertinent to our discussion are—

Subsec. (a): *Computation of Taxable Income — Taxable income shall be computed on the basis of the taxpayer's taxable income.*

Subsec. (b): *Taxable year — The term "taxable year" means—*
(1) the taxpayer's annual accounting period, if it is a calendar year or a fiscal year;
(3) the period for which a return is made, if . . . for a period of less than 12 months.

Subsec. (c): *Annual Accounting Period — The annual period on the basis of which the taxpayer regularly computes his income in keeping his books.*

In a shorthand way, we depict the principles above in Figure 6.1.

When selecting an accounting year, C corporations have more latitude than do S corporations. A C corporation needs only to establish a natural business cycle that is representative of the industry at large, for its type of business. Once a fiscal year is established, stringent rules apply to prevent distortion of IRS revenue when seeking to change such year.

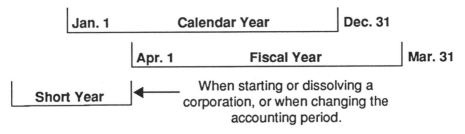

Fig. 6.1 - The Taxable Year: Any Consecutive 12 Months

An S corporation, because it passes through its net income to shareholders, is expected to use a calendar year. This is the substance of Section 1378: *Taxable Year of S Corporation.* However, a "permitted year" may be—

any other accounting period for which the corporation establishes a business purpose to the satisfaction of the [IRS].

In other words, a fiscal year can be selected for S corporations. But this can be done only if a "natural business year" can be established which does not significantly distort shareholders' income.

Change of Tax Year

In theory, a corporation — whether C or S — has indefinite life. As such, it is expected to maintain its selected or permitted tax year without change. But when a business experiences significant change in its "natural business cycle," a change in tax year can be made. For this change, the approval of the IRS is required. Section 442: *Change of Annual Accounting Period,* states—

If a taxpayer changes his annual accounting period, the new accounting period shall become the taxpayer's taxable year only if the change is approved by the [IRS]. [Emphasis added.]

The "only if" is addressed in Regulation § 1.442-1(b)(1), namely:

In order to secure prior approval of a change of . . . annual accounting period, the taxpayer must file an application on

*Form 1128 . . . . Approval will not be granted unless the taxpayer . . . establishes a **substantial business purpose** for making the change, . . . including the tax consequences therefrom. Among the nontax factors that will be considered . . . is the effect of the change on the taxpayer's annual cycle of business activity. . . . The [application] agreement . . . shall . . . provide terms, conditions, and adjustments necessary **to prevent a substantial distortion of income** which otherwise would result from the change.* [Emphasis added.]

In other words, if a change is sought that clearly defers a substantial portion of income, or shifts a substantial portion of deductions, the Form 1128 application will not be approved. Nor will it be approved if the short period created (between old and new tax years) creates a substantial net operating loss or a substantial long-term capital gain. However, if a C corporation has not changed its tax year within 10 years, or if an S corporation reverts from a fiscal year to a calendar year, no Form 1128 is required. Form 1128 is titled: ***Application to Adopt, Change, or Retain a Tax Year.***

Dominance of Section 446

With respect to everyday matters of accounting, Section 446 dominates your "rules of engagement" with the IRS. While tax year matters are important, they are not so all-pervasive and all-intrusive as is Section 446: *General Rule for Methods of Accounting.* This tax law was first enacted in 1954 and has only been amended twice since that time (in 1977 and in 1984). It is the fallback rule on which the IRS relies when it disputes the adequacy of your books and records when on a revenue hunt.

Section 446 consists of approximately 300 words of statutory text. The most significant of these words are as follows (with emphasis added):

Subsec. (a): ***General Rule*** — *Taxable income shall be computed under the method of accounting on . . . which the taxpayer **regularly computes his income** [when] keeping his books.*

Subsec. (b): ***Exceptions*** — *If no method of accounting has been regularly used . . ., or if the method used does not clearly reflect income, the computation of taxable income shall be made under such method as, in the opinion of the* [IRS], *does **clearly reflect income.***

Subsec. (c): ***Permissible Methods*** — *A taxpayer may compute taxable income under any of the following methods—*
 (1) *the cash receipts and disbursement method;*
 (2) *an accrual method;*
 (3) *any other method permitted; or*
 (4) *any combination of the foregoing methods permitted under regulations.*

Subsec. (d): ***Engaged in More than One Business*** — *A taxpayer engaged in more than one trade or business, **may**, . . . use a different method of accounting for each trade or business.*

Subsec. (e): ***Requirement re Change of Method*** — *A taxpayer who changes the method of accounting on . . . which he regularly computes his income in keeping his books **shall**, before* [using] *. . . a new method, **secure the consent** of the* [IRS].

Subsec. (f): ***Failure to Request Change of Method*** — *If the taxpayer does not file with the* [IRS] *a request to change the method of accounting, the absence of the consent of the* [IRS] *. . . shall not be taken into account . . . (1) to prevent the imposition of any penalty, or the addition of any amount to tax.*

The above statutory words (about 215) are interpreted via numerous regulations, revenue rulings, and court decisions. There are approximately 270 pages of such regulations and rulings; they comprise approximately 186,000 words! Obviously, there is no way that we can convey in a few scholarly words the full impact of

Section 446. The best that we can do is to touch on only some of its highlights.

Must Clearly Reflect Income

The emphasis in Section 446 is accounting for income: less so for deductions. The term "income" means the *total gross income* for the accounting year. To the IRS, that which clearly reflects income is that which establishes the highest total income possible. For a corporation, a clear reflection of income is that which produces the lowest total income. This, then, defines the accounting arena for endless disputes when your corporation's tax return is selected for IRS audit.

Regulation § 1.446-1(a): *General rule*, puts the above in better perspective. Its paragraph (2) reads in full—

*It is recognized that no uniform method of accounting can be prescribed for all taxpayers. Each taxpayer shall adopt such forms and systems as are, in his judgment, best suited to his needs. However, no method of accounting is acceptable **unless, in the opinion of the** [IRS], **it clearly reflects income**. A method of accounting which reflects the consistent application of generally accepted accounting principles in a particular trade or business . . . **will, ordinarily, be regarded** as clearly reflecting income, provided all items of gross income and expenses are treated consistently from year to year.* [Emphasis added.]

Paragraph (4) of the above regulation goes on to say—

*Each taxpayer is required to make a return of his taxable income for each taxable year, and **must maintain** such accounting records as will enable him **to file a correct return**. . . . [Such] records include the taxpayer's **regular books of account** and such other records and data as may be necessary to support the entries on his books of account and on his return.* [Emphasis added.]

Thus, the clear-reflection-of-income concept requires that the corporation keep honest, fair, and straightforward books and records. The premise is that, if the methods used turn out to be improper, an impartial analysis of the books will enable the proper method to be established. Whatever hand-entry system or computer program you use must be used consistently each year. The general principles involved above are summarized in Figure 6.2.

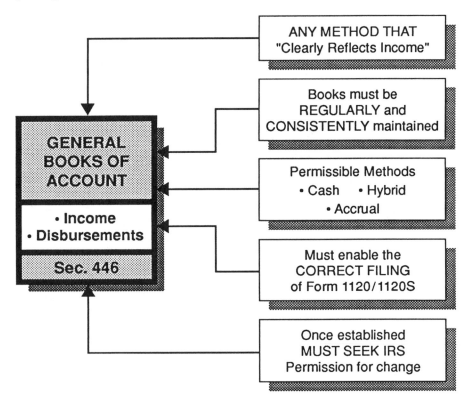

Fig. 6.2 - The "Clear Reflection of Income" Rule for Books of Account

If no books or records are kept, or if kept and they show material distortions of income — such as unexplained bunchings and spreadings — the IRS can ignore such records and impose its own method of accounting. An IRS-imposed method is guaranteed to produce the highest taxable income conceivable.

Cash vs. Accrual Methods

The IRS looks at your books for one of two general methods of accounting. There is the cash method or there is the accrual method. In some situations, a hybrid cash/accrual method may be permitted. This is common knowledge among bookkeepers and accountants. Corporate managers also possess this knowledge. But, often, managers try to finesse the books to achieve results more to their liking.

Under the cash method, income is reported in the year that it is actually or constructively received. Income is constructively received when an item is credited to one's account, is set apart, or is otherwise made available for the recipient's use. The form of income may be cash, cash equivalent, or property with an ascertainable fair market value. Cash equivalents include checks, notes, credits, letters of credit, forgiveness of debt, assumption of liabilities, or any other form of easily negotiable item. Disbursements are entered in the books when actually paid in cash or paid in cash equivalents. We call this process the "checkbook method": cash in, cash out. It is straightforward and simple.

Tax accounting simplicity is not the real goal of the Internal Revenue Code. Its and the IRS's goal is the collection of maximum revenue which is deemed correct. The consequence is that the cash method is subject to statutory limitations in certain cases. This is so ordained by Section 448: *Limitation on Use of Cash Method.* The essence is that—

> *In the case of a (1) C corporation, (2) partnership which has a C corporation as a partner, or (3) tax shelter, taxable income* **shall not be computed under the cash receipts and** *disbursements method of accounting.*

With one exception, the clear mandate is that C corporations must use the accrual method whether they like it or not.

Subsection 448(b)(3): *Entities with gross receipts of not more than $5,000,000* provides an exception to the accrual mandate. If the average annual gross receipts of a C corporation do not exceed $5,000,000 during the most recent three taxable years, the cash method may be used. S corporations can use the cash method regardless of gross receipts. Nevertheless, any corporation whose gross receipts regularly exceed $5,000,000 (5 million) per year will be pressured by the IRS to use the accrual method.

Under the accrual method, the legal right to receive income, rather than its actual receipt, determines when an amount is included in gross income. This method particularly favors the IRS. If a corporation ships out merchandise or performs services, then bills its customer/client for the full amount due, the billing amount is treated as income. This is so whether the billed amount is eventually received or not, or received in extended payments, or receivable only after extensive litigation is pursued. The end result is that, in many cases, tax is paid on money which is not yet in the corporate treasury. This is called: *forward taxing*. No wonder the IRS loves accrual accounting. It gets its revenue ahead of all others, including the taxpayer.

Also under the accrual method, disbursements are entered on the books only in the year in which all events have occurred that establish the fact of corporate liability for payment. The "all-events test" is not met until items have been purchased, delivered, accepted, and correctly invoiced. Whether the invoice is paid at that time or later is not the point. The moment that property, goods, or services come under your use and control, you have a legal obligation to pay for them. It is at that time that you have an IRS-recognized disbursement event. By timing your disbursement events (accounts payable) to closely match your income events (accounts receivable), it is possible to achieve a pseudo-cash method effect.

Inventory Capitalization

Inventory accounting methods differ significantly from the cash/accrual general rule. Such methods are covered in Code Sections 263A and 471 through 474. Section 263A: *Capitalization and Inclusion in Inventory Costs of Certain Expenses*. This is a real spoiler of conventional inventorying practices. It includes in inventory all of direct and indirect costs of design, manufacture, purchasing, storage, sales, shipping, and handling, including the proportionate share of insurance, utilities, rent, security, carrying charges, and other normally overhead items. Section 263A is a statutory club for locking up as much capital as possible into inventory. The 263A goal is to keep capital locked up until the inventory is either sold, damaged, liquidated, or junked.

Section 263A consists of over 4,000 words of text, and is accompanied by 370 pages (about 260,000 words) of regulations, revenue rulings, and court decisions. It was enacted in 1986 and is directed towards—

(1) *Real or tangible personal property produced by the taxpayer, and*

(2) *Real or tangible personal property acquired by the taxpayer for resale* [Sec. 263A(b)].

From a small C or S corporation's point of view, there are only two exceptions that are significant. There is a "small producer" exception and a "small reseller" exception. The small producer exception is found in Regulation 1.263A-1(b)(12): *De minimis rule for certain producers with total indirect costs of $200,000 or less.* This de minimis rule treats such producers as having no additional Section 263A costs. One could probably extend this de minimis amount to $500,000 without attracting the attention of the IRS. Especially so, under our definition of a "small corporation" (less than $5,000,000 in gross sales).

The small reseller exception is cited in subsection 263A(b)(2)(B): ***Exception for taxpayer with gross receipts of $10,000,000 or less.*** This subsection reads in part—

[Section 263A] *shall not apply to any personal property acquired . . . for resale if the average annual gross receipts of the taxpayer . . . for the 3-taxable-year period ending with the taxable year preceding* [the at-issue taxable year] *do not exceed $10,000,000.*

If the above two exceptions do not apply to your corporation, the next recourse is to pursue "simplified procedures" for the allocation of Section 263A costs. These procedures are set forth in—

Reg. § 1.263A–2(b): *Rules relating to property produced by the taxpayer; Simplified production method.*

Reg. § 1.263A–3(d): *Rules relating to property acquired for resale; Simplified resale method.*

These rules are based on formulating an "absorption ratio" which is applied to Section 471 costs. Be cautioned, however, that none of these rules is truly simplified.

Section 471 is titled: ***General Rule for Inventories.*** This rule permits judgmental latitude in—

*conforming **as nearly as may be** to the best accounting practices in the trade or business as most clearly reflecting the income* [thereof].

The term "as nearly as may be" permits estimates for shrinkage, if confirmed by physical count on a consistent annual basis. The implication of this section is that you do the best that you can to account for all costs associated with your inventory on hand at the end of each taxable year. As you'll see in a moment, you are permitted several options for valuing such inventory.

Valuing Ending Inventory

What the IRS is gunning for primarily is the dollar value of ending inventory at the close of each taxable year. The higher this value is, the lower the cost of goods sold. The lower the cost of goods sold, the higher the gross profit (for a known amount of gross sales). And, subsequently, the higher your taxable income (for a known set of operating expenses).

Using simple numbers for illustration purposes, the IRS's "end game" goes like this—

1. Gross sales $100,000
2. Beginning inventory   25,000
3. Purchases   15,000
4. Cost of production   20,000

5.	Sec. 263A costs	10,000	
	Subtotal	70,000	
6.	Ending inventory (1)	30,000	
	" " (2)	40,000	
	" " (3)	50,000	
7.	Cost of goods sold (1)		40,000
	" " (2)		30,000
	" " (3)		20,000
8.	Gross profit (1)		60,000
	" " (2)		70,000
	" " (3)		80,000

The IRS wants you — your corporation, that is — to use ending inventory (3): the highest value in our illustration above. In case (3), your gross profit would be $80,000. On the other hand, your accountant would like to use ending inventory (1): the lowest value illustrated. In case (1), your gross profit would be $60,000. This is $20,000 less than what the IRS would like to tax you on.

All of which brings us to the menu of checkboxes and questions directed at you, when preparing Schedule A of Form 1120/1120S. Said schedule is titled: *Cost of Goods Sold.* Your attention there is directed to the instruction—

Check all methods used for valuing closing inventory:

In edited form, we list for you in Figure 6.3 all such methods.

Note particularly in Figure 6.3 that three different regulations are referenced. These are—

Reg. § 1.471-2: *Valuation of inventories:* 2(c) *writedown of "subnormal" goods.*

Reg. § 1.471-3: *Inventories at cost.*

Reg. § 1.471-4: *Inventories at cost or market, whichever is lower.*

There is also reference in Figure 6.3 to the LIFO (Last-In, First-Out) method for valuing ending inventory. This method is very sophisticated, and is "big corporation" oriented.

Schedule A	COST OF GOODS SOLD	Form 1120 1120S

1. Inventory **beginning**   **2.** Purchases   **3.** Production   **2.** Sec. 263A

5. Other Costs   **6.** Total   **7.** Inventory **Ending**   **8.** Cost of goods sold

Check all methods used for valuing closing inventory:

(1) ☐ Cost as per Reg.§ 1.471-3

(2) ☐ Lower of cost or market as per Reg. § 1.471-4

(3) ☐ Other; specify & attach explanation _____

(4) ☐ Writedown of "subnormal" goods: Reg. § 1.471-2(c)

(5) ☐ If LIFO method adopted, attach Form 970

(6) ☐ If LIFO, enter percentage (or amounts) _____

(7) Do the rules of Sec. 263A apply   ☐ yes ☐ no

(8) Any changes in quantities, cost, or   ☐ yes ☐ no
     valuations between the beginning/ending?

● If "yes", attach explanation _____

Fig. 6.3 - "Check-the-Box" Aspects of Inventory Valuation

Unless you carry a quite substantial end-of-year inventory — say in the range of $1,000,000 or so — we suggest that you check only boxes (1), (2), or (3), and possibly (4), in Figure 6.3. Box (3) could be a *weighted-average cost* on a per unit basis. Box (4) is an opportunity to write down unsalable goods at normal prices . . . *because of damage, imperfections, shop wear, changes of style, odd or broken lots, and secondhand goods.* As long as your valuation analysis is reasonable and consistent, and can be explained in a one-page attachment, the IRS will generally accept methods (3) or (4) by small C and S corporations.

7

BALANCE SHEET BALANCING

Schedule L Consists Of Three Listings Of Items: ASSETS (14), LIABILITIES (6), And STOCKHOLDERS' EQUITY (5). All Data Entered Must Derive From General Books Of Account. At The End, Total Assets MUST EQUAL Total Liabilities Plus Stockholders' Equity. When Balance Not Achieved, "Adjustments to Equity" Become The Wedge Item Of Choice. The Reconciliation Of Income/ Expenses PER BOOKS With Income/ Deductions PER RETURN Uses Schedule M-1. Up To $250,000 In Retained Earnings Is Allowed With Schedule M-2(C). Previously Taxed Income Can Be Retained, When Schedule M-2(S) Is Used.

On Form 1120 (for C corporations) at the headblock portion, there is an entry space marked "D". Its caption is: *Total assets* $_____. Similarly, on Form 1120S (for S corporations), the space is marked "E". Its caption also is: *Total assets* $_____. The dollar amount that is entered into these spaces comes from Schedule L at the line marked "15": *Total assets*. Said amount is an indicator of the size of the corporation and its seriousness of entrepreneurial activity.

Schedule L appears on page 4 of Form 1120/1120S. This is the back page of the preprinted official form. Its title is: *Balance Sheets per Books*. The term "per books" means as determined by the accounting method regularly used in maintaining the corporation's general books of account. Recall Chapter 6.

Schedule L consists of three separate accounting portions designated as: Assets, Liabilities, and *Stockholders' Equity*. Among these three items, a "balancing act" is involved. The total assets (at the beginning and ending of each taxable year) MUST EQUAL the total liabilities and stockholders' equity for that year.

Below Schedule L, there are—

Schedule M-1: *Reconciliation of Income per Books with Income per Return*

Sched. M-2 (for C corporations): *Analysis of Unappropriated Retained Earnings per Books*

Sched. M-2 (for S corporations): *Analysis of Accumulated Adjustments Account, Other Adjustments Account, and Shareholders' Undistributed Taxable Income Previously Taxed*

These subschedules require beginning and ending balancing acts of their own. They also require reconciliation with Schedule L.

In this chapter, therefore, we want to touch on the highlights and intrigue of balancing Schedule L, and its associated reconciliation and analysis subschedules. While Schedules L and M for corporations with total assets less than $5,000,000 are seldom scrutinized by the IRS, said schedules comprise an essential element in the "financials" of a well managed company. The other essential element is the operating profit or loss for the current year. This "P & L" (also called: "E & P" — earnings and profits) is usually that which appears on page 1 of Form 1120/1120S. Hence, we want to tie together page 1 (front) and page 4 (back) of Form 1120/1120S in a meaningful and instructive way.

Clarification of Bad Debts

One of the commonly misunderstood items on pages 1 and 4 of Form 1120/1120S is the treatment of bad debts. It appears on page 1 in the *Deductions* block at the line captioned: *Bad debts*. It also appears on page 4 in the *Assets* block at the line captioned: *Less allowance for bad debts*. In both cases, where there is an entry for bad debts, there is a write-off benefit. Said benefit is allowed, however, only when it is clearly established that the debt is uncollectible or only partially collectible. All businesses have a collection problem with accounts receivable and trade notes outstanding more than 90 days.

For tax purposes, there are two classes of bad debts: business and nonbusiness. A business bad debt is one which is: (a) *created or acquired* in connection with a trade or business; or (b) *incurred* in a trade or business. All others automatically are classed as "nonbusiness" bad debts. Different rules apply. Business bad debts are deductible in full (if wholly worthless) or deductible in part (if partially worthless). Such is the essence of IRC Section 166: *Bad Debts*. Corporations are treated automatically as incurring business bad debts. This explains the preprinted entries on pages 1 and 4 of Form 1120/1120S.

Regardless of the business classification of a bad debt, it is not prima facie deductible . . . unless. The "unless" is its inclusion in income and in accounts receivable. For a cash method corporation, the bad debt would not be in income, though it might be carried on the books as "accounts receivable." For an accrual method corporation, the bad debt would be included in *both* income and in accounts receivable.

There was a time, prior to 1986, where corporations were allowed to charge off a "reserve" for bad debts on Schedule L. No more. Except for banks and savings and loan institutions, the only bad debt charge-offs allowed are those where it is clearly established that the debt is uncollectible or partly so. When so, the *specific charge-off* method is allowed. Thus, when a debt is known truly to be bad — say, after 90-plus days of persistent demands and followups — the debt can be written off where it is included in income and/or in accounts receivable. If, subsequently, the debt or part of it is repaid, the amount received is entered as "other income" on your corporation's books and on its return.

Asset Listing Review

In Chapter 3, we introduced you to Schedule L: *Balance Sheets per Books*. We did so with Figure 3.6. Because we need that figure again, we are repeating it here as Figure 7.1. At this point, we

Schedule L	BALANCE SHEETS PER BOOKS		
	Assets • Beginning/end of tax year	**C Corp**	**S Corp**
1	Cash on hand		
2	Accounts receivable		
3	Inventories		
4	U.S. Government obligations		
5	Tax exempt securities		
6	Other current assets		
7	Loans to stockholders		
8	Mortgage & real estate loans		
9	Other investments		
10	a. Buildings & other appreciable assets		
	b. Less accumulated depletion	< >	< >
11	a. Depletable assets		
	b. Less accumulated depletion	< >	< >
12	Land (net of any amortization)		
13	a. Intangible assets (amortizable only)		
	b. Less accumulated amortization	< >	< >
14	Other assets		
15	**TOTAL Assets**		
	Liabilities & Stockholders' Equity	**C Corp**	**S Corp**
16	Accounts payable		
17	Mortgages, notes, bonds payable (less than 1 yr)		
18	Other current liabilities		
19	Loans from stockholders		
20	Mortgages, notes, bonds payable (1 yr or more)		
21	Other liabilities		
22	Capital stock a. preferred		/////
	b. common		
23	Additional paid-in capital		
24	Retained earnings - Appropriated		/////
25	Retained earnings - Unappropriated		
26	Adjustments to stockholders' equity		
27	Less cost of treasury stock	< >	< >
28	**TOTAL Liabilities & Stockholders' Equity**		

Fig. 7.1 - Items Comprising a "Balance Sheet" on Tax Forms 1120/1120S

call to your attention the 14 assets that are listed in Figure 7.1. Except for accounts receivable (asset #2) and minor editing, the listing shown in Figure 7.1 is identical with that on the official Forms 1120 and 1120S.

On an official Schedule L, asset #2 reads as—

Trade notes and accounts receivable _____
• Less allowance for bad debts   ≤ _____ ≥

As explained above, there is no longer any "allowance" (or reserve) for bad debts. Under the specific charge-off method, the bad debt is deductible at any time during the taxable year. Thus, when the end of the year accounting comes, no allowance or reserve is needed. The write-off has already been taken. Hence, there is no deduction line in our Figure 7.1 for asset #2.

The overall official instruction to Schedule L simply reads—

The balance sheets should agree with the corporation's books and records.

No other significant instructions are given. This is because most of the 14 assets listed are reasonably self-explanatory.

Less self-explanatory, perhaps, are: *Other current assets* (#6), *Other investments* (#9), and *Other assets* (#14). The term "other" on a tax return always means other than that which fits on a preprinted line. Asset #6, for example, refers to any form of demand loan, promissory note, or specific pledge or guarantee which is time dated and fixed in principal amount. Asset #9 refers to marketable securities in other corporations and partnership ventures. Asset #14 refers to refunds, rebates, discounts, credits, and other amounts legally due the corporation but not yet actually received. On the official form, there is a parenthetical instruction: *attach schedule*, for entries on these three asset lines.

Asset #13: *Intangibles less amortization*, is often misleading. The term "intangibles" applies to expenditures for organizational costs, leasing fees, covenants not to compete, trademarking company name, and other intangibles which have been acquired by purchase or contract. Self-created intangibles such as goodwill, systems in place, customer lists, etc. are not entered on Schedule L. This is because the cost for creating such intangibles has been written off as an ordinary operating expense of the corporation.

Now, the Liabilities Side

The asset items on Schedule L are usually the most understood and best documented aspects of the corporation. The head accountant wants the books to reflect as many positive things about the company that he can. It is the liability side of Schedule L where the records tend to be incomplete, poorly substantiated, and garbled. Part of this uncertainty is due to the fact that the term "liability" also includes *Stockholders' Equity*. The term "equity" is the net worth of the corporation (assets minus liabilities). Such equity belongs to the stockholders and, because so, it is an accounting liability only. It is not a legal liability in the creditor demand sense. The stockholders are the risk takers at all times. Unfortunately, in closely held C and S entities, the principals consider all other persons as the risk takers, but not themselves.

For the moment, let us separate out the stockholders' equity items in Figure 7.1. When we do so, we have six corporation liability items, namely: 16 through 21. In synoptic form, we highlight these items, as follows:

Item #16: *Accounts payable* — these are those payables which are generated through ordinary trade or business activities with suppliers, vendors, subcontractors, lessors, etc.

Item #17 *Mortgages, notes, bonds, etc.* (short-term) — these are those payables due in less than one year to commercial lenders of all types, including long-term obligations paid down to one year remaining.

Item #18 *Other current liabilities* (attach schedules) — these are payables due in less than one year for non-commercial loans, insurance coverage, unpaid utilities, rent arrears, etc.

Item #19 *Loans from stockholders* — use extreme caution here. Are they truly "loans," or are they disguised contributions of capital that the corporation needs?

Item #20 *Mortgages, notes, bonds, etc.* (long-term) — these are payables due in more than one year for mortgages on real property, vehicle and equipment installment contracts, revolving lines of credit, and other long-term commercial indebtedness.

Item #21 *Other liabilities* (attach schedule) — best reserved for delinquent taxes, licenses, permits, and regulatory fees. The term "taxes" as a liability does **not** include income taxes, but does include payroll taxes, property taxes, sales taxes, and excise taxes (where applicable). These are priority type liabilities which, in a well managed corporation should be zero or nearly so. The "nearly so" applies to those delinquencies not paid within 30 days after the close of the taxable year.

If the above six liability items were properly recorded on the company books and properly managed, they would constitute the *Total liabilities* of the corporation. Unfortunately, there is no separate subtotal entry line on Schedule L for this purpose as there is for *Total assets*. Nevertheless, let us imagine that there is a separate subtotal liabilities line on Schedule L. When subtracting the subtotal liabilities from the total assets, the result would be the *Net Worth* of the company. The net worth should be a separate entry on your worksheets that support Schedule L. Thereupon, the net worth becomes the balancing target for establishing stockholders' equity.

Stockholders' Equity

As an aid to where we are heading on Schedule L, we present Figure 7.2. It is a simple 3-box block diagram. The end goal of Schedule L is to have the sum of boxes 2 and 3 equal box 1. The sum of boxes 2 and 3 is captioned on Schedule L as: *Total*

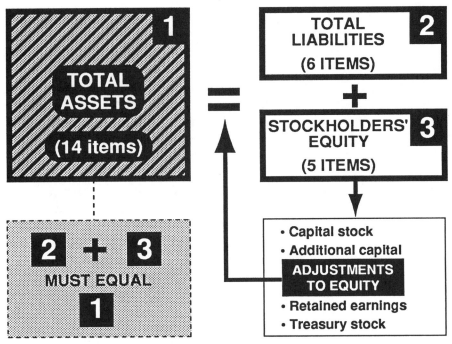

Fig. 7.2 - Balancing Role of "Adjustments to Equity" on Schedule L

Liabilities and Stockholders' Equity. It is the stockholders' equity portion of Schedule L that we want to now address. As indicated in Figure 7.2, there are five elements comprising stockholders' equity, namely: (1) capital stock, (2) additional capital, (3) adjustments to equity, (4) retained earnings, and (5) treasury stock. Note that we show "adjustments to equity" as the adjusting wedge for balancing Schedule L.

Refer for a moment back to Figure 7.1 on page 7-4. At item #22: *Capital stock*, you'll see the first of two distinctions between C and S corporations with respect to Schedule L. Whereas C corporations can issue *Preferred* and/or *Common* stock to its shareholders, an S corporation can issue only common stock. In either case, stock is issued only when capital (or its equivalent) is contributed to the corporation's enterprise. The total amount of capital stock issued should be posted and certified in the Shareholders Ledger. We discussed the importance of this ledger in Chapter 1, and summarized its contents in Figure 1.3 (on page 1-

11). Thus, for a given total number of shares issued, the amount of capital contributed should be more or less fixed.

Item #23 (in Figure 7.1): *Additional paid-in capital*, should also be in the Shareholders Ledger. Said amount represents additional capital contribution by existing shareholders, when no additional shares are issued to said contributors. Instead of there being "loans" from stockholders (item #19), the IRS looks more favorably upon additional paid-in capital. This additional capital **adds** to the cost basis of each individual's shares already held. Thus, for a given total number of shares issued, the additional capital paid in may be — most likely will be — disproportionate to each individual's share holdings.

Items #24 and #25 (in Figure 7.1) are captioned: *Retained earnings*. This is the second distinction between C and S corporations on Schedule L. For C corporations, there are two categories of retained earnings: *Appropriated* and *Unappropriated*. The term "appropriated" means pursuant to a formulated plan that covers the anticipated needs of the business. For S corporations, the distinction between the appropriated/unappropriated retained earnings is less significant (than for C corporations). We'll explain why, below. Meanwhile, all retained earnings comprise the stockholders' total equity in the business.

Item #26 (in Figure 7.1): *Adjustments to stockholders' equity*, is just that. It is an "adjustment" to make the balance sheet balance. In many cases, no rational explanation can be given. It is an adjustment necessary to make the total liabilities plus total equity equal the total assets of the corporation. As such, this is the **last entry** that should be made on the liabilities side of Schedule L. Think of it as a balancing facilitator or adjustment "wedge." In some cases, as implied in Figure 7.2, it is a pure force fit of the data.

Accumulated Earnings

The retained earnings entered on Schedule L are, in reality, the accumulations of undistributed earnings which have not been taxed as dividends. For C corporations, these retained earnings are classed as undistributed dividends. When said amounts are not distributed to stockholders, they are not income taxed to them. As a consequence, the implication arises that there is an attempt to avoid tax at the shareholder level, even though the C corporation itself pays tax on the retained earnings.

For S corporations, the retained earnings situation is quite different. Such earnings constitute *un*distributed taxable income: not undistributed dividends. By virtue of the pass-through feature of S corporations, the retained earnings **are taxed** at the shareholder level, even though said earnings are not actually distributed to them. Count on S shareholders to complain vigorously when they pay tax on money they do not receive. Yet, there are times when anticipated business needs require that some of the taxable earnings be retained. For an S corporation using Schedule M-2 (to be described later) the retention is characterized as: *Undistributed taxable income previously taxed.* Hence, the special accumulated earnings rules that apply to C corporations do not apply generally to S corporations.

There is a batch of special rules in the Tax Code designated as Subchapter G: *Corporations Used to Avoid Income Tax on Shareholders*. This grouping title alone implies that Congress, the IRS, and the Tax Court are fully aware of the tax sheltering maneuvers practiced by closely held entities. To discourage these maneuvers, there are seven rules which we cite as follows:

Sec. 531 — Imposition of Accumulated Earnings Tax
Sec. 532 — When Subject to Accumulated Earnings Tax
Sec. 533 — Evidence of Purpose to Avoid Income Tax
Sec. 534 — Burden of Proof
Sec. 535 — Accumulated Taxable Income
Sec. 536 — Income Not Placed on Annual Basis
Sec. 537 — Reasonable Needs of Business

Although S corporations are not specifically exempted from Sections 531 through 537, it is pretty clear in Section 532(a) that unless there are C corporation carryovers into S status, S corporations are not . . .

formed or availed of for the purpose of avoiding the income tax with respect to its shareholders . . . by permitting earnings and profits to accumulate instead of being divided or distributed.

The combined essence of Sections 531 through 537 is that a 39.6% **surtax** is imposed on accumulated earnings in excess of $250,000 [Sec. 535(c)(2)(A)]. This $250,000 amount is a base allowance, before the surtax attaches. In a C corporation, this base allowance applies to *Retained earnings — Unappropriated* (item #25 in Figure 7.1).

Over and above the $250,000 base allowance, *Appropriated retained earnings* are allowable. These are amounts expressly set aside for meeting anticipated — and duly planned — reasonable needs of the business. The term "reasonable needs" [Sec. 537] is described in Regulation § 1.537-2(b) as providing for—

(1) expansion of the business
(2) replacement of equipment
(3) procurement of inventory
(4) product liability insurance
(5) retirement of bona fide indebtedness
(6) extraordinary working capital

. . . and so on. These needs must be spelled out in a board of directors' resolution, and the information communicated to shareholders.

Personal loans to shareholders and to friends of shareholders, or investments in properties and securities unrelated to the regular business of the corporation are summarily disallowed. Unallowed appropriated retentions revert to "unappropriated" retentions subject to the 39.6% surtax. The whole purpose of this surtax is to dissuade the majority interests from using a C corporation as a tax avoidance umbrella.

Treasury Stock Explained

Item #27 (in Figure 7.1) is captioned: *Less cost of treasury stock*. This raises the questions: What is treasury stock and what is meant by "less cost of"?

Treasury stock is the buying back from an existing shareholder (who paid money for it) all or part of his shares. The bought-back shares are retained by the corporation where they are available for re-issue. In small corporations, the buyback is usually triggered by internal reasons, such as death of a shareholder, reduction of ownership say in management, payoff in the case of a threatened lawsuit, and the quieting of vociferous dissension.

Money for the buyback most often comes out of retained earnings unappropriated, or out of retained earnings in general. This explains the "less cost of" portion of the treasury stock caption. The buyback amount paid becomes a subtraction from the Schedule L retained earnings. It is so signified by the bracket symbols < > in Figure 7.1 (on page 7-4).

Any payment to a stockholder out of retained earnings gives the impression that the payments are in lieu of dividends. Distributed dividends, as you know, are shareholder taxable as ordinary income. If the payment distribution is a bona fide redemption of stock, preferential capital gain treatment applies. A bona fide redemption requires that some *meaningful reduction* in ownership interest takes place after the buyback. This is the premise on which Section 302: *Distributions in Redemption of Stock*, comes into play.

The essence of Section 302 is that, if certain conditions are met, the distribution from retained earnings can be treated as an *exchange*, where the capital gain/loss rules apply. The "certain conditions" are enumerated in subsection 302(b): *Redemptions Treated as Exchanges*. There are four such conditions, namely:

(1)   Redemptions not equivalent to dividends, and
(2)   Substantially disproportionate redemption of stock; or
(3)   Termination of shareholder's interest; or
(4)   Redemption in partial liquidation of the corporation.

Condition (4) is a stand alone. Conditions (1) and (2) have to be considered together, as do conditions (1) and (3). The term "substantially disproportionate" in condition (2) means a *reduction* in ownership interest of 20% or more after the buyback compared to ownership interest before the buyback. For example, if one owned 32% of the corporation's voting stock, to be considered a redemption rather than a distribution of dividends, his ownership interest after the buyback would have to be 25.6% or less [0.32 x (1 − 0.20)]. This 20% reduction-of-ownership rule applies only to minority shareholders: those holding less than 50% of the corporation's stock.

For majority shareholders, the reduction in ownership interest must leave that shareholder with less than 50% of the stock. For example, if one held 65% of the stock before a redemption, a 20% reduction would reduce his holdings to 52% [0.65 x (1 – 0.20)]. The payments to him would be dividends: not a redemption. To qualify as a redemption (say, to 49% ownership), the percentage of reduction in ownership would have to be 24.6% [1 – 0.49/0.65].

By following the rules of Section 302 and its regulations, the buyback of treasury stock can be a valuable tool for internal management purposes. As such, it is useful in both C and S corporations.

Schedule M-1: Reconciliations

On Form 1120 (for C corporations) and on Form 1120S (for S corporations), below Schedule L, there is Schedule M-1. This schedule is titled: *Reconciliation of Income (Loss) per Books with Income (Loss) per Return*. The same title is used, whether it be a C or S corporation. The contents of Schedule M-1 for C and S corporations are similar but different. We display the contents (as edited) and the C-S differences in Figure 7.3. We are using the C corporation M-1 as our base of reference.

Schedule M-1 is a good tool for tracking down — called: *reconciliation of* — the income/expense differences between your corporation's books and its returns. As is always the case in real life, the accounting methods used and the tax law on income inclusions/exclusions and deduction allowances/disallowances will never exactly match each other. While Schedule M-1 is not a prerequisite to the completion of Schedule L: *Balance Sheets per Books*, it can be helpful in discovering where corrections and adjustments need to be made to Schedule L.

The only instructions on Schedule M-1 focus your attention on travel and entertainment (T&E) items. You are referred to IRC Section 274: *Disallowance of Certain Entertainment, etc., Expenses*. The instructions outline 10 types of T&E items which may be entered on the corporation's books as an expense, which are

Schedule M-1	RECONCILIATION OF INCOME / Loss per books WITH INCOME / Loss per return		Form 1120 1120S	
		S		S
1. Net income/loss per books		√	7. Income recorded on books not included "on return"	√
2. Federal income tax		X		
3. Excess capital losses over gains		X	• Tax-exempt interest	√
			• Other (itemize)	
4. Income "subject to tax" not recorded on books (itemize) ----------		√	---------- ---------- ---------- ----------	
			8. Deductions on return not charged against book income	√
5. Expenses recorded on books not deducted on return		√	a. Depreciation	√
			b. Contributions carryover	X
a. Depreciation		√	c. Other (itemize)	
b. Travel & entertainment		√	---------- ----------	
c. Contributions carryover		X	---------- ----------	
d. Other (itemize)			9. Add lines 7 & 8	√
---------- ----------			10. Income/loss > line 6 less line 9	√
6. Add lines 1 through 5		√		

Notes: √ means same as C corporation
X does not apply to S corporation
"subject to tax" for C means "on Schedule K" for S
"on return" for C means "on Schedule K" for S
Line 10. Must equal "Taxable income" on page 1, Form 1120
Line 10. Must equal "Income/loss" on Schedule K, Form 1120S

Fig. 7.3 - Schedule M-1: Reconciliation Differences: S vs. C Corporation

not allowed in full or not at all, on your return. Otherwise, most of the items on Schedule M-1 are fairly self-explanatory.

As indicated in Figure 7.3, item #1 is: *Net income(loss) per books*. This is NOT the same as *Taxable income*/(loss) on page 1 of Form 1120, nor *Ordinary income*/loss on page 1 of Form 1120S. Items #2 and #3 apply only to C corporations. Item #4 is functionally comparable between C and S, except for the S corporation reference to Schedule K (for pass-through items).

Similarly for item #5, except that there are no "contributions carryover" for S corporations. Items #7, #8, and #9 are comparable for C and S corporations. Item #10 in Figure 7.3 should equal the Taxable income on Form 1120, and should equal the Ordinary income on Form 1120S. This bottom line equality between books and return suggests that item #10 should be entered first. Item #1 should be entered second. Then use the blank lines at items #4 and #7 for income adjustments, and the blank lines at items #5 and #8 for expense/deduction adjustments.

Schedule M-1 is a balancing act of its own: separate from that of Schedule L. It becomes a real challenge in the panic and rush when closing the books — and the return — for the taxable year. Always do the best that you can, and "force fit" when necessary. Over the course of five or 10 years any bona fide inconsistencies tend to wash themselves out.

Schedule M-2: C Corporations

On Form 1120, there is a Schedule M-2 at the very bottom of its page 4. It is below Schedule M-1 which is below Schedule L. The title of Schedule M-2 is: *Analysis of Unappropriated Retained Earnings per Books*. This title also includes reference to: *Line 25, Schedule L*. The caption to said line is: *Retained earnings — Unappropriated*. (Recall Figure 7.1, item #25.) For most C corporations, there is an accumulated earnings *credit* of $250,000 [Sec. 535(c)(2)(B)]. This means that if the retained earnings – unappropriated exceed this amount, a 39.6 percent surtax applies (per Section 531). Management, therefore, tries to take advantage of the $250,000 of retained earnings that are not surtaxed.

Schedule M-2 is a straightforward continuous accounting of the unappropriated retained earnings. It is simple and self-explanatory, as evident in our Figure 7.4. The accumulated earnings at the beginning and ending of each year posted on Schedule M-2 must match the corresponding entries on Schedule L.

There is a tax message in Figure 7.4. It is that management has the prerogative at any time during the year to declare dividends and make distributions to the stockholders. By anticipating the cumulative amount at the end of the year, dividend distributions can

Form 1120	CORPORATION INCOME TAX RETURN	Page 4

| Schedule L | BALANCE SHEETS PER BOOKS Fig. 7.1 | |

| Schedule M-1 | RECONCILIATION OF INCOME PER BOOKS WITH RETURN Fig. 7.3 | |

| Schedule M-2 | ANALYSIS OF UNAPPROPRIATED RETAINED EARNINGS per Books & Line 25, Schedule L | |

1. Beginning of year		5. Distributions	
2. Net income/loss *		a. cash b. stock	
3. Other increases (itemize) ---------- ---------- ----------		c. property	
		6. Other decreases (itemize)	
		7. Add lines 5 & 6	
4. Add lines 1,2, & 3		8. End of year	
* per books		Line 4 less line 7	

Fig. 7.4 - Format & Contents of Schedule M-2 for C Corporations

be made so as to keep the Schedule M-2 ending balance at less than $250,000. This provides an allowable tax shelter cushion for unanticipated needs of the business.

With regard to anticipating the operating needs of a C corporation (upgrades and improvements, replacement of obsolete equipment, Treasury stock buy-backs, etc.), there is no $250,000 retained earnings limitation. Such is the consequence of Section 537: *Resonable Needs of the Business.* The nonlimitation aspect is implied on Schedule L (in Figure 7.1) at item **#24**: *Retained earnings - Appropriated.* The amount "appropriated" is determined by reference to the *Bardahl* formula [*Bardahl Mfg. Corp.*, 24 TCM 1030, Dec. 27,494(M), TC Memo, 1965-200]. This "formula" is used by the IRS and the Tax Court for computing the working capital needs, both ordinary and extraordinary, throughout a full-year operating cycle. Section 537 applies also to S corporations.

Schedule M-2	ANALYSIS OF "CARRYOVER ACCOUNTS" FROM C STATUS; S STATUS PTI ACCOUNT		Form 1120-S
ITEM	(a) * AAA Account	(b) * OAA Account	(c) * PTI Account
1 Beginning of tax year			
2 Ordinary income, page 1		/////	/////
3 Other additions			/////
4 Ordinary loss, page 1	< >	/////	/////
5 Other reductions	< >	< >	/////
6 Combine lines 1 through 5			
7 Nondividend distributions			
8 End of tax year			
/// Subtract line 7 from line 6	/////	/////	/////
*	AAA = Accumulated Adjustments Account OAA = Other Adjustments Account PTI = Shareholders' Undistributed Taxable Income Previously Taxed		

Fig. 7.5 - Format & Contents of Schedule M-2 for S Corporations

Schedule M-2: S Corporations

There is also on Form 1120S a Schedule M-2 for S corporations. This M-2 serves an entirely different purpose from that of a C corporation's M-2. There are carryover accountings from C to S status, when applicable, and the retention of previously taxed income for anticipated business needs. Consequently, the Schedule M-2(S) consists of three special subaccountings, namely:

(a) Accumulated adjustments account (AAA)
(b) Other adjustments account (OAA)

     (c)   Shareholder's undistributed taxable income previously taxed (PTI).

The format and contents of this schedule are presented in Figure 7.5.

The instructions for Schedule M-2(S) are quite complex. For the AAA and OAA accounts (columns (a) and (b) in Figure 7.5), the emphasis is on accounting for the carryovers from a C corporation to an S corporation. The carryovers include the C corporation's accumulated earnings and profits, tax-exempt interest, and the book adjustments for federal income taxes. The complexity of this accounting can be minimized by the S corporation making one or both of two elections, namely:

- *Election to distribute accumulated earnings and profits,* or
- *Election to make a deemed dividend.*

These elections could virtually eliminate the AAA account altogether, and materially reduce any entries in the OAA account. This would leave the PTI account as the primary focus for pure S corporations.

The beauty of the PTI account (column (c) in Figure 7.5) is that all affected shareholders have to consent. They do so by attaching a statement to the S corporation's return: *Election to Forego PTI.* The term "affected shareholder" means any shareholder to whom a prorata distribution of ordinary income has been assigned during the taxable year. By paying ordinary tax on this amount and by foregoing its actual distribution from the PTI account, each consenting shareholder's tax basis in his S corporation stock is enhanced. Thereafter, the PTI account is available to management (as retained earnings) for meeting bona fide business needs. Any unused PTI can be distributed later as nontaxable return of capital.

8

CAUTIONS RE PHC STATUS

In Addition To Regular Tax On Ordinary Business Income Of A Corporation, There Is A 39.6% PHC Tax On UNDISTRIBUTED Personal Holding Company Income. Items Covered By This Tax Are: Dividends, Interest, Rents, Royalties, Income From Personal Service Contracts, And The "Free Use" Of Company Property By Shareholders. If The Total PHC Income Equals Or Exceeds 60% Of The Corporation's ADJUSTED Ordinary Gross Income, AND 5 Or Fewer Individuals Own 50% Or More Of Its Stock, PHC Status Exists. The Most Practical Way To Reduce The PHC Tax Is To Distribute The PHC Income As Dividends.

The letters PHC stand for: *Personal Holding Company*. This is a domestic C-type corporation in which five or fewer shareholders control 50% or more of the value of the corporation. Special constructive ownership rules apply which count all closely-related family members as one stockholder. PHCs, when properly structured, are useful for close-family and multi-family tax planning. A PHC uses the corporate shield, its various accounting techniques, and its special dividend deductions, to meter out tax benefits to passive participants in the corporation's investment affairs.

A PHC is also a C corporation from which at least 60% of its adjusted gross income is derived from passive activities, such as: dividends, interest, rents, royalties, annuities, etc. There is nil material participation by the owners and employees in ordinary trade or business affairs. It is regarded by the stockowners as a "holding" corporation for their lucrative investments . . . worldwide.

Why is a PHC so tax different from an active trade or business C corporation?

Answer: Because a special PHC tax applies: IRC Section 541. This section is titled: ***Imposition of Personal Holding Company Tax***. The imposition is a 39.6% surtax—

> ***In addition*** *to other* [C corporation] *taxes . . . each taxable year on the* **undistributed** *personal holding company income (as defined in section 545).* [Emphasis added.]

In this chapter, therefore, we want to acquaint you with the special PHC rules that apply, particularly with regard to defining PHC income and how it is computed. In the process, we have to tell you about the constructive ownership-of-stock rules in Section 544. There are ownership counting surprises for you in said section. Certainly, we want to acquaint you with Schedule PH (Form 1120) for computing the surtax, and why S corporations are not PHC qualified. There can be confusion of a PHC with a PSC (Personal Service Corporation), but we'll try to make the distinction clear. When prudently used, a PHC can combine the benefits of both an active trade or business with passive investment activities.

S Corporations Unaffected

An S corporation, by its own statutory definition (Section 1361) is a small *business* corporation. This means that the employees and owner-employees materially participate in the ongoing activities of the trade or business. The "business" is one in which consumer products are designed, produced, and sold, and related services thereto performed. Although an S corporation can engage in investment activities not related to its core business, there are no special incentives for doing so.

If the S shareholders wanted to engage more prominently in passive investment activities, the corporation would have to qualify as an SBIC: Small Business Investment Company. To do so, it would have to be licensed under the Small Business Investment Act of 1958, and offer its shares to the public. In contrast to an SBIC, an S corporation is limited to 75 shareholders whose shares are not registered for public trading.

If an S corporation does engage in portfolio-type investments, producing income in the form of interest, dividends, rents, royalties, capital gains and losses, etc. the resulting income is passed through automatically to the shareholders (Section 1366). The portfolio income cannot be retained by the corporation as undistributed accumulated earnings, as in the case of a C corporation. As we discussed in the latter part of Chapter 7, any consensus-retained earnings are classified as a PTI account (Previously Taxed Income). No PHC tax would apply as there would be no untaxed PHC income.

For investment diversity purposes, an S corporation can have any number of wholly owned subsidiaries that it wants. Each qualified S subsidiary can engage in a separate investment activity of its own. In the end, though, all net income generated by each subsidiary is funneled through the parent S corporation. This follows from subsection 1361(b)(3)(A)(ii): *Treatment of certain wholly owned subsidiaries—*

All assets, liabilities, and items of income, deduction, and credit of a qualified subchapter S corporation shall be treated as assets, liabilities, and such items (as the case may be) of the [parent] *S corporation.*

Thus, we are back to the primary characteristic of an S corporation. Except for certain built-in gains from prior C corporation status (if any), the S corporation itself is not income taxed. All forms of income — active, passive, or other — are passed through for taxing at the shareholder level. This pass-through feature alone removes such income from the definition of a PHC entity.

Avoid Confusion with PSC

A personal service corporation (PSC) is defined in Section 448(d)(2)(A) as—

Any corporation substantially all of the activities of which involve the performance of services in the fields of health, law, engineering, architecture, accounting, actuarial science, performing arts, and consulting.

A PSC is a corporation whose compensation for the performance of personal services is more than 50% of its total compensation income. Of this amount, more than 20% of the total compensation income must derive from employee-owners. An "employee-owner" is one who owns more than 10% of the fair market value of the corporation's outstanding stock.

Once a C corporation becomes a PSC, several statutory features take place. If not already on a calendar year accounting period, it must cease its fiscal year operations. Simultaneously, it is required to use the cash method for its books and records. These two features are intended to put PSCs on an accounting par with individuals who are also performing similar professional services in proprietorship, partnership, or S corporation form. In other words, a C corporation of professionals is not supposed to be used for skewing taxable income of its employee-owners in any special beneficial way.

There is another statutory change in a PSC compared with a regular trade or business C corporation. Whereas a C corporation may have an accumulated earnings credit up to $250,000 before the 39.6% surtax kicks in, a PSC is limited to $150,000. This lower amount is set by Section 535(c)(2)(B): *Minimum credit; Certain service corporations.*

As a result of the above changes, there is no incentive for using a PSC to accomplish PHC (mere holding and investment) goals. Still, there is a powerful advantage of a PSC for its professional members. Being a C corporation, it can have as employee-owners an association of shareholders who themselves are proprietorships, partnerships, S corporations, estates, and trusts. All of the separate "entities" are individual persons under the tax laws. Such an arrangement permits each shareholder-employee-professional to establish his own retirement and estate plans, independent of the C corporation's plans. In this manner, the C corporation provides retirement plan benefits to its nonowner employees, while providing health insurance and limited liability benefits to all employees.

Overview of PHC Statutes

The tax treatment of a personal holding company (PHC) necessitates the application of many tax laws. In addition to the general rules for C corporations, there is a gamut of special rules. These special rules start with Section 531: *Imposition of Accumulated Earnings Tax*, and extend through Section 565: *Consent Dividends*.

In a more focused arrangement in the Internal Revenue Code, Sections 531 through 565 are prescribed as **Subchapter G** of Chapter 1: *Normal Taxes and Surtaxes*. Subchapter G is titled: *Corporations Used to Avoid Income Tax on Shareholders*. From this subchapter title alone, there is a key message. The PHC rules are directed primarily at the *shareholders* who direct the company activities, rather than at the corporation itself. If you keep this one point in mind, you'll understand better the interpretive complications that can arise.

Subchapter G is structured into four parts, namely:

Part I — Corporations Improperly Accumulating Surplus
Part II — Personal Holding Companies
Part III — Foreign Personal Holding Companies
Part IV — Deduction for Dividends Paid

As for our part, we'll focus primarily on Part II, though we'll touch briefly on Parts I and IV when necessary and relevant.

As to Part II: Personal Holding Companies, the directly applicable sections are—

Sec. 541 — Imposition of personal holding company tax
Sec. 542 — Definition of personal holding company
Sec. 543 — Personal holding company income
Sec. 544 — Rules for determining stock ownership
Sec. 545 — Undistributed personal holding company income
Sec. 546 — Income not placed on annual basis

Sec. 547   — Deduction for deficiency dividends

As we've had to do in other chapters, we can touch only on the highlights of these sections which we think are most instructive.

PHC Income Defined

The PHC tax is 39.6% of the undistributed PHC income. As such, we need to focus on the substance of such income, as defined in Section 543. We caution you, however, that Section 543 does **not** provide any straightforward definitive explanation. The section consists of approximately 3,800 statutory words! It is one of those rare situations where the supporting regulations are fewer in word count (about 2,700) than the tax law itself.

The essence of the 3,800-word Section 543: *Personal Holding Company Income*, is its subsection (a): *General Rule*. In highly abbreviated form, subsection (a) says—

The term "personal holding company income" means the portion of the adjusted ordinary gross income which consists of:
- *(1)   Dividends, etc.*
- *(2)   Rents*
- *(3)   Mineral, oil, and gas royalties*
- *(4)   Copyright royalties*
- *(5)   Produced film rents*
- *(6)   Use of corporate property by shareholder*
- *(7)   Personal service contracts*
- *(8)   Estates and trusts.*

These are 43 out of approximately 1,600 words comprising the full text of subsection 543(a). Needless to say, we have overly abbreviated subsection (a). For example, the "etc." in item (1) includes—

*interest, royalties (other than mineral, oil, or gas royalties or copyright royalties) and annuities. This paragraph shall **not** apply to—*

(A) *interest constituting rent (as defined in subsection (b)(3)), . . . and*
(C) *active business computer software royalties (within the meaning of subsection (d)).*

Items (2) rents and (3) mineral royalties are not included in PHC income if—

The adjusted gross income from rents . . . [and] from mineral, oil, and gas royalties . . . constitutes 50 percent or more of the adjusted ordinary gross income.

Unless the core business of the corporation derives its income primarily from rental property and mineral rights, rental income and mineral royalties **are** included in the definition of PHC income. In the inclusion process, there are certain adjustments to rents (depreciation, taxes, interest) and to mineral royalties (depletion, taxes, interest). These adjustments are prescribed in subsection (b)(2)(A) for rents, and in subsection (b)(2)(B) for mineral royalties.

At this point, there are three sets of adjustments to the above listing of items included in PHC income. In Figure 8.1, we summarize all of the above inclusions, with modifications as appropriate. We believe that Figure 8.1 is more meaningfully instructive than our trying to cite the full text of Section 543(a).

Adjusted Ordinary Gross Income

The leadoff sentence in Section 543(a) employs the clause: *the portion of adjusted ordinary gross income which consists of . . . .* This raises the question: What does "adjusted ordinary gross income" mean? To answer this question, you have to know the meaning of "gross income," and the meaning of "ordinary gross income."

The term *Gross income,* is defined by Section 61(a). It means *. . . all income from whatever source derived . . .* within the U.S. or without the U.S. if derived from a domestic corporation.

	PERSONAL HOLDING COMPANY INCOME		
1	Dividends		
2	Interest		
	• **Less**: Adjustments *	< >	
3	Royalties (other than minerals, etc.)		
4	Annuities		
5	Rents		
	• **Less**: Adjustments *	< >	
6	Mineral, oil, & gas royalties		
	• **Less**: Adjustments *	< >	
7	Copyright royalties		
8	Produced film rents		
9	Compensation for use of entity property		
10	Personal service contracts		
11	Income from estates & trusts		
12	**PHC income**: Add lines 1 through 11		☐
	* Attach schedule. Otherwise, see instructions.		

Fig. 8.1 - Items Comprising PHC Income for Testing Purposes

The term *Ordinary gross income* is defined by Section 543(b)(1). This term means—

The gross income determined by excluding—
    (A) all gains from the sale or disposition of capital assets,
    (B) all other gains from the sale or disposition of section 1231 property [used in the trade or business of the corporation], *and*
    (C) all . . . [non-U.S. PHC] *income of a foreign corporation . . . other than that received for personal service contracts or the sale thereof* [to be performed in the U.S.]

The term *Adjusted ordinary gross income* is defined by Section 543(b)(2). This term means—

The ordinary gross income adjusted as follows:
  (A) Rents . . .
  (B) Mineral royalties . . .
  (C) Interest . . .
  (D) Certain excluded rents . . .

The point here is that there are four sets of adjustments to ordinary gross income before arriving at the "adjusted" ordinary gross income. We portray the whole sequence for you in Figure 8.2.

	ADJUSTED ORDINARY GROSS INCOME		
1	Gross income (from all sources)		
2	**Less:** Capital & other gains		< >
3	**Ordinary gross income**, Combine 1 & 2		
4	Adjustments:	/////	
	a	Deductions allocable to rents	
	b	Deductions allocable to royalties	
	c	Deductions allocable to compensation	
	d	Certain excluded interest income	
5	Total adjustments. Add 4a through 4d		< >
6	**Adjusted ordinary gross income** Subtract line 5 from line 3		
/////	See instructions for required adjustments.		

Fig. 8.2 - Items for Establishing Adjusted Ordinary Gross Income

The 60% PHC Income "Test"

Section 542(a): Definition of PHC; General Rule, says—

The term "personal holding company" means any corporation other than . . .

  (1) an exempt organization,
  (2) a bank,
  (3) a life insurance company,

SMALL C & S CORPORATIONS

    (4)   a surety company,
    (5)   a foreign PHC,
    (6)   a lending or finance company,
    (7)   a foreign corporation,
    (8)   a small business investment company,
    (9)   a corporation in bankruptcy, and
  (10)   a passive foreign investment company.

When the "other thans" are out of the way, there are two tests for determining whether a corporation is a PHC or not. In short title form, these two tests are:

(A)   the 60% PHC income test, **and**
(B)   the 50% stock ownership test.

Both of these tests must apply concurrently for the taxable year at issue, before the 39.6% surtax applies.

As to test (A), subsection 542(a)(1) must be gone through. The long title of this test is: *Adjusted Ordinary Gross Income Requirement.* In pertinent part, this test reads—

Any corporation . . . if . . . at least 60 percent of its adjusted ordinary gross income [Fig. 8.2] *. . . for the taxable year is personal holding company income* [Fig. 8.1].

We were preparing you for this 60% test when we presented Figures 8.1 and 8.2.

The mathematics is simple. You *divide* the PHC income at the bottom of Figure 8.1 by the adjusted OGI (ordinary gross income) from Figure 8.2, and express the result as a percentage. The formula goes like this:

$$\frac{\text{PHC income}}{\text{Adjusted OGI}} = \frac{\text{Fig. 8.1}}{\text{Fig. 8.2}} = \underline{\hspace{1cm}}\%$$

For example purposes, consider that the XYZ corporation receives $50,000 in ordinary income, $75,000 in dividends, $165,000 in rents, and $35,000 in capital gains for the taxable year.

8-10

The rent adjustments are $95,000 (for depreciation, mortgage interest, and property taxes). What is the test percentage of PHC income? It is $75,000 dividends plus $70,000 [165,000 − 95,000] adjusted rents. These items come to $145,000 [75,000 + 70,000]. This follows the sequence in Figure 8.1.

The gross income consists of $50,000 in regular business income, plus $75,000 dividends, plus $165,000 rents, plus $35,000 capital gains for a total of $325,000. The ordinary gross income (OGI) is $325,000 less the $35,000 in capital gains. This comes to $290,000. Adjusting this amount for the $95,000 for rents, the "adjusted" OGI comes to $195,000 [290,000 − 95,000]. This follows the sequence in Figure 8.2.

As per the formula above, divide the $145,000 in PHC income by the $195,000 of adjusted OGI. The result comes to 0.7435 or 74.35%. Since this percentage is *at least 60 percent* (Sec. 542(a)(1)), the XYZ corporation is potentially a PHC. Before it can be declared so, the stock ownership test must be examined.

The 50% Ownership Test

The second test of a PHC is the *Stock Ownership Requirement*: Section 542(a)(2). The opening sentence of this section reads—

At any time during the last half of the taxable year more than 50 percent in value of its outstanding stock is owned, directly or indirectly by or for not more than 5 individuals.

Note that the ownership involves four separate elements, namely: (i) last 6 months of the taxable year, (ii) 50% or more in value, (iii) directly or indirectly by or for, and (iv) not more than 5 individuals.

Why the last six months of the taxable year? Because experience shows that by the time the third operating quarter (9 months) comes around, the income mix — PHC and ordinary — is more or less defined. This enables the controlling interests to rearrange the stock ownership more to their liking, before the end of the tax accounting year.

Note that the "50% or more" term expressly mentions: *in value*. It is not 50% or more of total shares nor 50% or more of voting shares. The ownership test is 50% or more of the total value of the outstanding stock of the corporation. In a C corporation, various classes of preferred and common stock can be issued with different par values and different voting rights. It is the fair market value of the corporation as a unit — as if it were sold — that establishes its "in value" amount. The question then is, how many outstanding shares represent the more-than-50% amount?

The clause *directly or indirectly by or for* gets us into the stock ownership rules of Section 544. We'll get to this section shortly below. This clause recognizes the reality that in closely held corporations a founder, over time, tends to dilute his appreciating ownership interests by selling, exchanging, gifting, or otherwise transferring nonvoting shares to members of his immediate family and close relatives. The founder still maintains his initial relative control over the corporation. In this kind of situation, the founder has both direct ownership of stock (*by* himself) and indirect ownership (*for* himself).

The *not more than 5 individuals* seems clear enough. Still, it is clearer when you recognize that the term "individual" includes certain entities. S corporations, partnerships, estates, and trusts which are shareholders in the corporation are also treated as individuals. This is due to the pass-through feature of these entities to a designated individual. Pass-through entities are often used by controlling interests of a small C corporation to further dilute their individual taxation consequences. There is nothing illegal about this. But for PHC purposes, entity dilution does not avoid the 50% ownership test.

Constructive Ownership of Stock

Section 544 of the IR Code is formally titled: *Rules for Determining Stock Ownership*. Its primary thrust is subsection (a): *Constructive Ownership*. This subsection reads in part—

For purposes of determining whether a corporation is a personal holding company:

(1) Stock not owned by individuals — *Stock owned, directly or indirectly, by or for a corporation, partnership, estate, or trust shall be considered as being owned proportionately by its shareholders, partners, or beneficiaries.*

(2) Family and partnership ownership — *An individual shall be considered as owning the stock owned, directly or indirectly, by or for his family or by or for his partner . . . . The family of an individual includes only his brothers and sisters (whether by whole or half blood), spouse, ancestors, and lineal descendants.*

Let us exemplify paragraph (2) above. Consider that the following numbers of shares are held by the following members and close relatives:

	shares		shares
An individual	40 (√)	His son's half-sister	40
His father	100 (√)	His brother's wife	10
His wife	20 (√)	His wife's father	20
His brother	10 (√)	His wife's brother	10
His son	20 (√)	His wife's brother's wife	50
		Total shares outstanding	320

How many shares does the individual constructively own?

Answer: 190 shares. We have indicated these by (√). He actually owns only 40 shares, or 12.5% (40 ÷ 320). Yet, he controls 190 shares, or 59.4% (190 ÷ 320).

This is a good illustration of how the total number of shares outstanding can be "diluted" among family members and close relatives, while retaining more than 50% control over those shares.

Overview of Schedule PH

If it turns out that: (1) 5 or fewer individuals control more than 50% of the stock ownership, **and** (2) the dividends, etc. comprise 60% or more of the adjusted ordinary gross income, the requirements of Section 542(a) are met. By this statutory definition the corporation is a PHC (Personal Holding Company). As such, attention to three other matters is required.

The first item of attention is to signify to the IRS that your corporation is a PHC. This is done by checking the appropriate box in the left-hand head portion of Form 1120, which reads:

A. Check if a:

    2. Personal holding co. (attach Sch. PH)   ☒

By checking box 2, the IRS is put on notice that a 39.6% surtax is included in the overall tax computation for the corporation.

The second item of attention is to prepare and attach Schedule PH to the corporation's Form 1120. The full title of this schedule is: ***U.S. Personal Holding Company (PHC) Tax. See separate instructions. Attach to tax return.*** This is a 2-page form, segregated into six parts. It accommodates 50 separate line entries. Strictly for overview purposes, we show in Figure 8.3 the partitioning aspects of Schedule PH (Form 1120). If it appears that your corporation is lapsing into a PHC status, having an official copy of this schedule and its instructions is an experience of its own.

What we haven't told you previously is that our Figure 8.1 is actually Part II of Schedule PH. The PHC income test is the first of two tests prescribed in Section 542(a)(1): ***Adjusted ordinary gross income requirement.*** Nor have we told you previously that our Figure 8.2 is an edited version of the Worksheet contained in the instructions for figuring the adjusted ordinary gross income.

The instructions to the Worksheet represented by our Figure 8.2 say—

> *Keep for your records . . . . If* [the result] *is **60% or more** and the Stock Ownership Requirement . . . is met, the corporation is a PHC . . . . Complete Part IV.*

Part IV consists of stating the names and addresses of the **five** highest percentage controlling shareholders, during the last half of the taxable year.

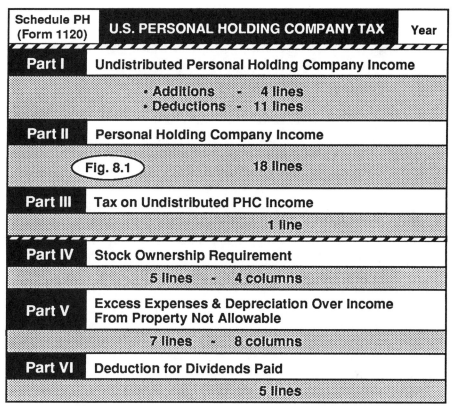

Fig. 8.3 - General Arrangement of Schedule PH (Form 1120)

The third item of attention is to enter the PHC tax in Part III of Schedule PH. This involves just one entry line. Its caption and instructions read—

PHC tax. *Enter 39.6% of line* _____ [captioned: Undistributed PHC income] *here and on Schedule J (Form 1120), line* _____ [captioned: Personal holding company tax].

Schedule J (Form 1120) is the tax computation summary — of some 20 checkboxes and 15 entry lines — that comprise the upper half of page 3 of Form 1120. The PHC tax is only one of the 15 line entries that make up the *Total tax* on Schedule J.

Computing Undistributed PHC Income

The 39.6% PHC tax applies only to the *undistributed* PHC income. The implication is that, if the PHC income is distributed, the PHC tax does not apply. This is not totally true. The undistributed amount is figured as though it were individual income and not corporate income. Certain deductions allowable to corporations are not allowable to individuals and, to some extent, vice versa. The differences between the tax treatment of individuals and of C corporations are prescribed in the 1000-word Section 544: *Undistributed Personal Holding Company Income*.

The PHC tax computation starts with the tentative taxable income shown on page 1 of Form 1120. This is the amount of corporate taxable income *before* two special deductions apply (for the regular tax). These two deductions — (a) net operating loss and (b) special dividends — are *added back* as PHC income. There is no special dividend deduction for individuals, as there is for corporations. The net operating loss deduction is also treated differently for individuals.

So, too, are "excess expenses and depreciation" added back into the PHC computational process. Said expenses and depreciation are those which pertain to the excess over the actual rental income derived from real estate and tangible property owned by the corporation. For individuals, no such excess is allowed whereas for corporations it is allowed.

Charitable contributions comprise another item where there are different deductible limits between corporations and individuals. For corporations, the contributory limit is 10% of its taxable income. For individuals, the limit is 50% of one's adjusted gross income. As a result, for undistributed PHC income purposes, corporate charitable contributions for individuals are subtracted out.

To see the effect of this add-back-then-subtract-out feature, we call to your attention line 2 (add back) and line 6 (subtract out) in Figure 8.4. Our Figure 8.4 is an edited version of Part I of Schedule PH. As you may note, it is divided into two computational portions: *Additions* and *Deductions*. As we have emphasized at line 13 in Figure 8.4, the end result of Part I of Schedule PH is:

		UNDISTRIBUTED PERSONAL HOLDING COMPANY INCOME		
Additions	1	Taxable income before special deductions		
	2	Contributions deducted in line 1		
	3	Excess expenses & depreciation, from part V		
	4	Total. Add lines 1 through 3		
Deductions	5	Federal income and other taxes not deducted		
	6	Contributions deductible as an individual		
	7	Net operating loss for preceding year		
	8	Net capital gain from Schedule D		
		Less: Income tax on net gain	< >	
	9	Deduction for dividends paid, from part VI		
	10	Total. Add lines 5 through 9		
	11	Subtract line 10 from line 4		
	12	Dividends paid after end of tax year		
	13	**Undistributed PHC income.** Subtract line 12 from line 11		

Fig. 8.4 - Items for Computing Amount of Undistributed PHC Income

Undistributed PHC income. Once this amount is computed, the PHC tax is 39.6% of said amount. It is a flat tax, pure and simple.

Cheaper to Distribute

Although the PHC tax is computed as though the income were attributed to individuals, the tax is paid by the corporation. The 39.6% is maximum rate for individuals. For single individuals, this rate starts at about $280,000 of Form 1040 *taxable* income. For married individuals filing jointly, the maximum rate also starts at around $280,000 of taxable income. If all shareholders — including family members and close relatives of the controlling interests — had Form 1040 taxable incomes in excess of these amounts, it would be simpler for the corporation to pay the tax.

The more likely scenario, we believe, is that most shareholders would have individual rates from 15% to 36%. From a total PHC tax point of view, it would be cheaper to distribute the undistributed

PHC income. Indeed, this is the very purpose of the PHC tax. It is to induce the corporation to distribute rather than retain the PHC income in its corporate treasury.

Retained PHC income is not treated the same as retained earnings in the ordinary business income sense. As you may recall from Chapter 7, ordinary business retained earnings enjoy up to $250,000 as a credit base against the 39.6% accumulated earnings tax of Section 531. The PHC income component in the total retained earnings **does not participate** in the $250,000 nontaxable credit base.

Therefore, it behooves the controlling interests of a closely held C corporation to distribute the PHC income as dividends. If the corporation does this, it can get a deduction on its Schedule PH for the dividends paid. Such is the role of Part VI (Schedule PH) titled: *Deduction for Dividends Paid under Sections 561 and 562.* Section 561 defines this deduction as including—

(1)   the dividends [actually] *paid during the taxable year,*

(2)   the consent [hypothetical] *dividends for the taxable year, and*

(3)   the dividend carryover [excess dividends over income] . . . *from the two preceding taxable years.*

Section 562 sets the rules for determining the Section 561 amounts.

Of particular interest here are the "consent dividends" at item (2) above. The term *consent* means that the shareholders, while not actually receiving the dividends as in (1) and (3) above, consent to paying individual tax on said dividends. The consent dividends may then be retained by the corporation as after-tax working capital. For the consenting shareholders, the consent retains of PHC income are treated as *additional paid-in capital* on the corporation's balance sheet: Schedule L. Then each shareholder's basis in his stock is increased proportionally.

9

FOREIGN ACTIVITY QUESTIONS

All Income Tax Returns Of Shareholders (Forms 1040, 1041, And 1065) And Those Of C And S Corporations (Forms 1120 And 1120S) Ask Two "Must Answer" YES–NO Questions. One Question Asks About Foreign ACCOUNTS; The Other About Foreign TRUSTS. In Addition, Form 1120 Asks Each C Corporation About Its Being A 10% Or More Shareholder In A CONTROLLED Foreign Corporation. And About Its Having A 25% Or More Shareholder Who Is A Foreign Citizen Or Entity. All Except The Foreign Accounts Question IMPLY That Tax Evasion Is The Goal Unless Agonizing Special Forms Are Filed.

Whether you are an individual or a corporation, you report as gross income all income from sources worldwide. That is, the term "gross income" — when preparing a U.S. tax return — is not limited to sources within the U.S. This is clearly so implied in the statutory sentence—

all income from whatever source derived . . .

in IRC Section 61(a): *Gross Income Defined.*

As a consequence of this all-sweeping definition, very pointed questions appear on all income tax returns concerning foreign accounts, foreign trusts, and foreign corporations. The questions are not intended to imply any illegality in having one or more foreign accounts, nor are they invasion of your privacy. Congress has the power to make these inquiries to assure that all receipts of money or money equivalents are constitutionally taxable. So, don't be paranoid when you read the preprinted checkbox questions on your return. Answer them truthfully: ☐ Yes or ☐ No, as appropriate. Have all the foreign accounts you want; just disclose them when asked about them.

In this chapter, therefore, we want to familiarize you with the specific foreign account questions you are asked, what's behind the questions, and how you should answer them responsibly. For example, if the combined value of all of your accounts in a foreign jurisdiction was $10,000 or less at any time during the taxable year, you are instructed to answer "No". But if you answer "Yes", there is an associated tax form to prepare and submit. We certainly want to tell you about these tax forms so that you will not be caught off guard or be misunderstood. Trying to be too clever and secretive about foreign activities may not be in your best tax interests.

The Most Common Question

For our purposes, we designate the most common foreign accounts question as: Question 1. It is not so numbered on any of the applicable tax returns. Nevertheless, it appears on Form 1040 (for individuals), Form 1041 (for estates and trusts), Form 1065 (for partnerships) and Form 1120/1120S (for corporations: C and S). On each of these returns, except for the word "you," Question 1 is worded almost exactly the same. It is the location on each return where differences arise. We'll point out these locations to you as we go along.

Question 1 reads specifically as follows:

At any time during calendar year_____, did you have an interest in or a signature or other authority over a financial account in a foreign country, such as a bank account, securities account, or other financial account? ☐ *Yes,* ☐ *No.*

For individuals, this question appears on Schedule B (Form 1040) at Part IV: *Foreign Accounts and Trusts*. The preprinted instructions to this question read:

You must complete this part if you (a) had over $400 of interest or dividends; (b) had a foreign account, or . . .

The question is item 7 on Schedule B (1040), and is followed by: *See instructions for exceptions and filing requirements.*

For estates and trusts (Form 1041), Question 1 appears as item 3 in a section bold caption: **Other Information.** Instead of "you," the question asks: *. . . did the estate or trust have . . . .* The same "see instructions" words apply.

For partnerships (Form 1065), Question 1 appears as item 9 on Schedule B (1065): **Other Information.** The same "see instructions" words apply. The only noteworthy difference is that a prior question is asked:

Did this partnership have any foreign partners? ☐ *Yes,* ☐ *No.*

Foreign partners are U.S. taxed on their prorata share of income similarly to that for U.S. partners.

For corporations (Form 1120/1120S), Question 1 appears as item 8 on Schedule K (1120): **Other Information.** For S corporations, Question 1 appears as item 5 on Schedule B (1120S): **Other Information.** For both C and S corporations, the same "see instructions" words also apply.

The instructions define a foreign country as being any geographical area outside of the U.S., Guam, Puerto Rico, and the Virgin Islands. Furthermore, a "foreign account" is defined as—

Any bank, securities, securities derivatives, or other financial instruments accounts. Such accounts . . . also encompass [those] *in which the assets are held in a commingled fund, and the account holder has an equity interest in the fund. The term also means any savings, demand, checking, deposit, time deposit, or any other account maintained with a financial institution or other person engaged in the business of a financial institution.*

With this official definition of a foreign account, there is just no wiggle room for interpretive finessing. The only escape is if the aggregate value of all such accounts during *each calendar year* does not exceed $10,000 *at any time* during the calendar year. In such case, you can answer "No" to Question 1. Otherwise, if you — or your small C or S corporation — have any assets of any kind outside of the U.S. of which you have direct or indirect authority of any kind, you have to answer "Yes" to Question 1. Then you have to prepare and submit Form TD F 90-22.1.

Form TD F 90-22.1

When you answer "Yes" to Question 1, there are two things to do. The first is simple. Following the question, it says—

If "Yes", enter the name of the foreign country ▶ _____

If there is an account in more than one foreign country, you are required to enter separately each such country. The purpose in doing so is to identify whether a Tax Treaty is in effect between that country and the U.S. At present, there are about 62 foreign tax treaties in effect. If a foreign financial account is in a tax treaty country, there is less suspicion concerning a U.S. person's tax evasion activities there.

The second thing to do when answering "Yes" to Question 1 is to prepare and file Form TD F 90-22.1. Its title is: ***Report of Foreign Bank and Financial Accounts***. This is NOT a tax form. The IRS has nothing to do with this form, other than calling it to your attention when applicable. The letters on the form, "TD F" mean: Treasury Department — Foreign (account). Instructions on the form tell you **not** to file with your federal tax return. Instead, you file it with:

> U.S. Department of Treasury
> P.O. Box 32621
> Detroit, MI 48232-0621

The top portion of Form TD F 90-22.1 is Part I: ***Filer Information***. You enter such information as (1) Calendar Year, (2) Type of Filer: ☐ Individual ☐ Partnership ☐ Corporation ☐ Fiduciary, (3) Tax ID, (4) Name or Organization, (4) Address, (5)

Country, (6) Date of Birth (if an individual) or Date of Creation (if an entity), and (7) Title of Filer, as appropriate.

Part II of Form TD F 90-22.1 is where all of the financial disclosure action lies. Its title is: *Information on Financial Accounts*. Note the plural: Accounts. The first space in Part II is captioned:

> *Number of Foreign Financial Accounts in which a financial interest is held:* _____ .

The instructions tell you that for each separate account, whether in the same country or not, you must complete box spaces 1 through 6. You may also have to complete spaces 7 through 15. The instructions also say that—

> *If the filer holds a financial interest in more than 25 foreign financial accounts, indicate the number . . . and do not complete any further items in Part II.*

When more than 25 accounts, the U.S. Treasury Department will make immediate direct contact with you and/or your organization.

When 25 or fewer accounts, you are expected to provide the information in Figure 9.1 for *each* account on the same TD F 90-22.1 form for the calendar year. Page 2 of the form repeats the Figure 9.1 information three times. A preprinted headnote instruction there says—

> *This side* [page 2] *can be copied as many times as necessary in order to provide information on all accounts.*

Box space 3 of Figure 9.1 is quite interesting. It asks that you designate the maximum value of each account in U.S. dollars as—

a. ☐ Under $10,000
b. ☐ $10,000 to $99,999
c. ☐ $100,000 to $1,000,000
d. ☐ Over $1,000,000

TD F 90-22.1	REPORT OF FOREIGN BANK AND FINANCIAL ACCOUNTS	File With Treas. Dept. Detroit, MI

PART II | ACCOUNT INFORMATION   No. of accounts held ____

1. Type of account: ☐ Bank
   ☐ Securities ☐ Other _____

2. Account number or designation
   _____

3. Maximum value of account
   ☐ Under $10,000
   ☐ $10,000 to $99,999
   ☐ $100,000 to $1,000,000
   ☐ Over $1,000,000

4. Name of financial institution in which account is held

5. Country in which account is held

6. Does filer have a financial interest in this account?   If "No", complete boxes 7-15 *
   ☐ Yes ☐ No

7. Last name or Organization Name of Account Owner

8. First name	9. Middle Initial	10. **Tax** or other **ID** number _____
11. Address	12. City	13. State	14. ZIP

15. Country | Type of filer: ☐ Individual
   ☐ Corporation ☐ Other _____

Signature of filer	Date	Filing for calendar year

* If "yes", do NOT complete boxes 7-15.
● Complete same information for each separate account on Continuation Page hereof.

Fig. 9.1 - Treasury Dept.'s "Information Request" Re Foreign Accounts

The instructions as to "maximum value" indicate—

The largest amount of currency and non-monetary assets in the account at any time during the year. Convert foreign currency by using the official exchange rate at the end of the year, . . . or if withdrawn from the account, at the time of withdrawal.

The Next Common Question

All of the tax forms cited above (1040, 1041, 1065, and 1120/1120S) ask the same second question. As such, we designate it Question 2. In all cases, it appears immediately behind Question 1 on each return. We'll explain the reason for this in a moment. Accordingly, **Question 2** reads—

During the tax year, did you [the estate or trust, the partnership, or the corporation] *receive a distribution from, or were you the grantor of, or transferor to, a foreign trust?* ☐ *Yes* ☐ *No. If "Yes", you may have to file Form 3520.*

Whereas Question 1 is a foreign **accounts** question, Question 2 is a foreign **trusts** question. Question 1 applies when simply having any kind of financial account in a foreign country. No activity in or out of that account needs to take place. Simply having such an account requires a "Yes" answer.

Answering Question 2 is different. It is directed at a *reportable event* taking place during the year. Such event may be: (1) a distribution from, (2) a grant to (creation of), or (3) a transfer to . . . a trust arrangement in a foreign country. If there is no reportable event during the year, Form 3520 is not required. You answer "No" to the question.

If you are the responsible party for reporting the reportable event, the answer to Question 2 is "Yes". As the responsible party, Form 3520 is required. Form 3520 is a tax form whose IRS title is: *Annual Return to Report Transactions with Foreign Trusts and Receipt of Certain Foreign Gifts*.

Form 3520 is very formidable. It consists of six pages, 10 parts and subparts, about 60 Yes-No checkboxes, and approximately 120 entry spaces. In addition, it consists of 12 pages of two-columnar instructional text totaling approximately 10,000 words. The instructions direct that the form be filed in duplicate. Attach the original copy to your return; send the duplicate copy separately to—

Internal Revenue Service Center
Philadelphia, PA 19255

The Philadelphia Center is the world center for all trust activities in foreign countries by U.S. persons (individuals, partnerships, corporations, or others).

A bold printed headnote instruction to Form 3520 says—

All information must be in English. Show all amounts in U.S. dollars. File a separate Form 3520 for each foreign trust.

You are then asked to designate your U.S. person filing status as: ☐ Individual ☐ Partnership ☐ Corporation ☐ Trust ☐ Executor (of an estate). A "U.S. person" is a U.S. citizen, a U.S. entity, or a U.S. resident (whether a U.S. citizen/entity or not).

There is no way that we are going to attempt to step you through the mass of information required on Form 3520. The best we can do here is to depict in diagrammatic form the functional blocks of information required. We do this in Figure 9.2. Our diagram gives you the general idea involved. If Form 3520 is truly applicable to your situation, you will need the official form, its instructions, and — most likely — seasoned professional assistance.

Commentary on Foreign Trusts

Keep in mind that a U.S. person is also a domestic corporation (C or S) and all of its shareholders. The shareholders themselves may be individuals or entities (corporations, partnerships, trusts, or estates). When a U.S. person is involved, any transfer of money or property to, or distribution from, a foreign trust, is a U.S. tax accountable event. There is no escaping this fact.

Still, a common misperception prevails. There is belief that the controlling interests of a C or S corporation can quietly and privately arrange for the creation and administration of a foreign trust by a foreign trustee: a non-U.S. person or entity. It is believed that once this is done legally under the laws of the foreign jurisdiction, U.S. persons are thereafter free of all U.S. tax consequences and reporting. The income and property can be withdrawn at any time without the IRS being privy to each transaction. This seems to be

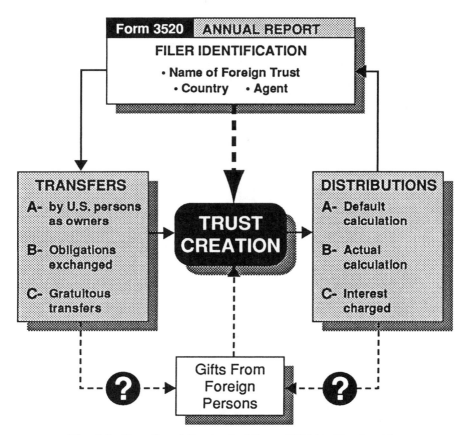

Fig. 9.2 - Functional Content of Form 3520 Re Foreign Trusts

the persistent dream among many successful small-business owners with grandiose world travel in mind.

Be introduced now to Section 679 of the Internal Revenue Code. This section is titled: ***Foreign Trusts Having One or More U.S. Beneficiaries***. Paragraph (1) of its subsection (a): ***Transferor Treated as Owner***, reads—

*A U.S. person who directly or indirectly transfers property to a foreign trust . . . shall be treated as the owner for his taxable year of the portion of such trust attributable to such property if for such year there is **a U.S. beneficiary of any portion** of such trust.* [Emphasis added.]

In other words, if a U.S. person wants to give his money or property to a foreign person or to a foreign entity, expecting nothing in return, that's O.K. It becomes a pure gratuitous transfer, classed as an international gift. If the transferee is an IRS-recognized foreign charitable organization, there are limited tax deduction benefits to the transferor.

But if there is just one person who is classed as a U.S. beneficiary of a foreign trust, the tax picture changes dramatically. Who is classed as a U.S. beneficiary? Section 679(c)(1): *Trusts Treated as Having a U.S. Beneficiary* states it this way—

For purposes of this section, a trust shall be treated as having a U.S. beneficiary for the taxable year UNLESS—

*(A) under the terms of the trust, **no part** of the income or corpus of the trust may be paid or accumulated during the taxable year for the benefit of a U.S. person, and*
*(B) if the trust were terminated at any time during the taxable year, **no part** of the income or corpus of such trust could be paid to or for the benefit of a U.S. person.* [Emphasis added.]

Thus, unless the trust instrument creating the entity expressly prohibits any and all distributions to U.S. persons, the distributees (whether natural born or foreign born, whether U.S. residents or nonresidents, whether individuals or entities) are automatically classed as U.S. beneficiaries. Furthermore, any foreign person (individual or entity) who participates in the trust arrangement as a nonresident alien, who subsequently becomes a U.S. resident within five years of a transactional event, automatically becomes a U.S. beneficiary [Sec. 679(a)(4)(A)].

You and your associates can dream and scheme, and hire all of the international tax attorneys you want, but you cannot escape the mandates of IRC Section 679. Once said section becomes applicable, Section 6048: *Information with Respect to Certain Foreign Trusts*, comes into play. Section 6048 is the statutory basis for Form 3520.

Our conclusion is that, unless there is a substantial and bona fide business need for a foreign trust, we see no point in it. Whatever your business financial needs may be in a foreign jurisdiction can be accomplished with a foreign account (rather than a foreign trust). Having a foreign trust when you do not really need one tends to raise suspicions of money laundering, tax evasion, and other illegal domestic and international activities.

C Corporations: Question A

In addition to the above two foreign situs questions for all U.S. persons and entities, C corporations have to respond to two other questions: A and B. On Form 1120, Question A immediately precedes Question 1 (the foreign accounts question), whereas Question B immediately follows Question 2 (the foreign trusts question). Both A and B questions appear on Schedule K: *Other Information*, on Form 1120.

Neither the A nor B question appears on Form 1120S for S corporations. By its tax definition [Sec. 1361(b)(1)(C)], an S corporation cannot have as one of its shareholders a nonresident alien (foreign person or foreign entity). An S corporation is a pure domestic entity, though it may engage in global business with reputably established import/export agencies. By contrast, a C corporation can have foreign shareholders, and also be a shareholder in a foreign corporation.

Accordingly, **Question A** on Form 1120 reads expressly as—

Was the corporation a U.S. shareholder of any controlled foreign corporation? (See sections 951 and 957.) ☐ *Yes,* ☐ *No.*

You need to look at IRC Sections 951 and 957 before answering "Yes" or "No". Section 951 defines a "U.S. shareholder"; Section 957 defines a "controlled foreign corporation." The tax meaning of the two terms is different from what your intuitive interpretations might otherwise be.

Section 951(b): *U.S. Shareholder Defined*, states that such term means—

*With respect to any foreign corporation, a U.S. person . . . who owns . . . or is considering owning . . . **10 percent or more** of the total combined voting power of all classes of stock entitled to vote of such corporation.* [Emphasis added.]

Recall that Question A asks — *Was the **corporation** [itself] a U.S. shareholder . . .?* The implication is that the C corporation is a domestic corporation. If it then holds 10% or more of the voting stock of a foreign corporation, it becomes a U.S. shareholder therein. If it holds *less than* 10% of a foreign corporation, it is not a U.S. shareholder. Question A is then answered "No".

The second part of Question A is: . . . *shareholder of any* **controlled** *foreign corporation.* Consequently, if the C corporation is a U.S. shareholder in a foreign corporation which is not a "controlled" foreign corporation, the answer to Question A is also "No". So, what is a controlled foreign corporation?

Section 957(a): ***Controlled Foreign Corporation***, says that the term "controlled" means—

*Any foreign corporation if **more than 50 percent** of—*

*(1) the **total combined voting power** of all classes of stock of such corporation . . . **or***
*(2) the total value of the stock of such corporation, is owned . . . or is considered owned . . . by U.S. shareholders on **any day** during the taxable year of such foreign corporation.* [Emphasis added.]

The phrase "total combined voting power," etc., is defined in Treas. Reg. § 1.957-1(b)(1)(i) as—

the power to elect, appoint, or replace a majority of that body of persons exercising . . . the board of directors [function] of such corporation.

In other words, if your corporation, together with one or more other U.S. persons, could influence more than 50% of the directors of a foreign corporation, it would be a U.S. controlled foreign corporation. Each U.S. shareholder thereafter (holding 10% or more of the foreign stock) would have to answer "Yes" to Question A. Having to answer "Yes" is **not** a good idea. Let us explain.

If "Yes" to Question A: Form 5471

The preprinted instruction immediately following Question A: ☐ Yes, ☐ No, reads—

If "Yes", attach Form 5471 for each such corporation. Enter number of Forms 5471 attached ▶ _____.

Have you ever heard of, or scanned, Form 5471?

Form 5471 is an IRS form titled: ***Information Return of U.S. Persons with Respect to Certain Foreign Corporations.*** Believe it or not, the form consists of nine pages plus four worksheet pages. Altogether there are over 250 line entries, some of which are columnized and some of which are boxed. There are 12 pages of 3-columnar instructions totaling approximately 26,000 words! Do you really want to get involved with such a form?

To give you a foretaste of what could be in store for you, we'll cite only the captions of the schedules and worksheets necessary to prepare Form 5471. These items are:

1. Filer Information (5 checkbox categories)
2. Schedule A: Stock of the Foreign Corporation
3. Schedule B: U.S. Shareholders of Foreign Corporation
4. Schedule C: Income Statement
5. Schedule E: Income, War Profits, and Excess Profits Taxes Paid or Accrued
6. Schedule F: Balance Sheet (of the foreign corporation)
7. Schedule H: Current Earnings and Profits
8. Schedule I: Summary of Shareholder's [Filer's] Income from Foreign Corporation
9. Schedule J: Accumulated Earnings & Profits of Controlled Foreign Corporation
10. Schedule M: Transactions between Controlled Foreign Corporations and Shareholders or Other Related Persons

11. Schedule N: Return of Officers, Directors, and 10% or More Shareholders of a Foreign Personal Holding Company
12. Schedule O: Organization or Reorganization of Foreign Corporation, and Acquisitions and Dispositions of its Stock
13. Worksheet A: Foreign Base Company Income and Summary of U.S. Shareholder's Pro Rata Share of Subpart F Income
14. Worksheet B: U.S. Shareholder's Pro Rata Share of Earnings of a Controlled Foreign Corporation Invested in U.S. Property
15. Worksheet C: U.S. Shareholder's Pro Rata Share of Previously Excluded Subpart F Income Withdrawn from Qualified Investments in Less Developed Countries.
16. Worksheet D: U.S. Shareholder's Pro Rata Share of Previously Excluded Export Trade Income Withdrawn from Investment in Export Trade Assets.

Shall we go on? Surely, you get the point. Congress and the IRS regard any investment in a controlled foreign corporation as an offshore tax avoidance device. Once so regarded, you cannot rely on "secrecy laws" of the foreign haven to protect against IRS examination of foreign-maintained documents [Sec. 982(b)(2)].

C Corporations: Question B

Question B on Form 1120 reverses Question A, to some extent. It is directed at foreign persons who are nonresidents of the U.S. being a shareholder in a U.S. corporation. With foreign persons the focus, Question B reads in full as:

At any time during the tax year, did one foreign person own, directly or indirectly, at least 25% of: (a) the total voting power of all classes of stock of the corporation entitled to vote, or (b) the total value of stock of the corporation?
☐ *Yes,* ☐ *No. If "Yes",*

    a. Enter percentage owned ▶ _____
    b. Enter owner's country ▶ _____
    c. The corporation may have to file Form 5472. Enter number of Forms 5472 attached ▶ _____ .

Form 5472 is in no way as inhospitable as Forms 5471 and 3520. It consists of $1^1/2$ pages plus $2^1/2$ pages of instructions. Altogether, it comprises about 24 lines, 35 box spaces, and about 12 checkboxes. Its IRS title is: ***Information Return of a 25% Foreign-Owned U.S. Corporation or a Foreign Corporation Engaged in a U.S. Trade or Business.***

Form 5472 is arranged into seven parts, namely:

Part I   —   Reporting Corporation
Part II   —   25% Foreign Shareholder
Part III   —   Related Party
Part IV   —   Monetary Transactions between Reporting Corporations and Foreign Related Party
Part V   —   Nonmonetary and Less-than-Full Consideration Transactions between the Reporting Corporation and the Foreign Related Party
Part VI   —   Additional Information

Form 5472 is not required if there is no reportable transaction in Parts IV and V. As per instructions, a "Reporting Corporation," is either:

•   *a 25% foreign-owned U.S. corporation, or*
•   *a foreign corporation engaged in a trade or business within the U.S.*

The instructions further say—

*A separate Form 5472 must be filed for each foreign or domestic related party with which the reporting corporation had a reportable transaction during the tax year. Attach Form 5472 to the income tax return **and** file a copy of Form 5472 with the Internal Revenue Service Center, **Philadelphia, PA 19255**.*

Concluding Commentary

From our discussion on Forms 3520, 5471, and 5472, it should be apparent that these forms are agonizing and time consuming. Especially so for a small business C corporation when participating unnecessarily in foreign financial activities.

Fact One is that, when participating in arrangements for a foreign trust, a U.S. controlled foreign corporation, or a foreign controlled U.S. corporation, a common thread comes through. That thread is the silent suspicion that some form of tax evasion is taking place. The suspicion is premised on the tax presumption of what takes place through related party transactions. Having a foreign person, foreign trust, or foreign corporation in the loop does not negate the suspicion. It only enhances it. We think that having a foreign account and filing Form TD F 90-22.1 is a better alternative

Fact Two is that, when a Form 3520, 5471, or 5472 is prepared, a separate copy is forwarded to the IRS Service Center in Philadelphia, PA. From this particular center, IRS revenue agents are dispatched to every U.S. Consulate Office throughout the world. Representatives of the foreign persons, trusts, or corporations (identified in the forms above) can be called to the Consulate Office for an IRS interview, or an IRS agent can visit the place of business of the foreign person or entity involved. The usual diplomatic outcome is some form of agreement from the foreign citizen or entity to cooperate with the U.S. in the administration of its tax laws.

Unless a foreign association is absolutely essential to the active trade or business of your domestic corporation, we think there is a better way to go. Do your foreign investing through U.S. brokerage firms which have international offices of their own. Invest in reputable foreign corporations whose stock is publicly traded. All dividends earned from these foreign sources are reportable to the IRS on Form 1099-DIV, and includible on Schedule C (Form 1120): *Dividends and Special Deductions*. Study the official instructions to Schedule C (1120) on the "special deductions" point. For small domestic corporations, the investment tax benefits of Schedule C are often overlooked.

10

ITEMS NOT DEDUCTIBLE

> Close Corporations Tend To Be Used For The
> Write-Off Of Personal, Living, Family, And
> Other Expenses Of The Controlling Interests
> (Officers, Directors, And 20% Owners).   IRC
> Sections 262, 264, 267, 274, And 280F
> Summarily Disallow Such Write-Offs.   Often,
> The Corporation Is Used As An Intermediary
> For Property Transactions, Million Dollar Life
> Insurance Policies, Lavish Entertainment, And
> Leasing Of Luxury Autos, Boats, Planes, Etc.
> For The Corporate Elite.   PERSONAL USE
> AFFIDAVITS Enable The Corporation To Assign
> About 25% Of Its Costs To The Gross Incomes
> Of Those Who Have Benefited.

One of the prevailing characteristics of a small C or S corporation is using the corporation as a tax shelter for the personal benefit of five or fewer controlling shareholders. Here the term "personal benefit" means writing off against the corporation such personal and family items as travel, entertainment, fancy cars, boats, airplanes, horses, vacation homes, repairs to residence, various insurance contracts, schooling of children, and so on.

These and other "so on" items are expressly identified in the Internal Revenue Code (IRC) as being **not deductible**. They are not deductible on the personal tax returns of the controlling shareholders, nor are they deductible as bona fide trade or business expenses of the corporation.

Altogether, there are 27 such items designated as nondeductible in Code Sections 261 through 280H. They appear in Part IX of

Subchapter A: *Determination of Tax Liability; Items Not Deductible*. The tone of the 27 nondeduction rules is set by the leadoff Section 261: *General Rule for Disallowance of Deductions*. This 21-word mandate reads in full as—

> *In computing taxable income **no deduction** shall **in any case be** allowed in respect of the **items specified** in this part* [Part IX]. [Emphasis added.]

Particularly note the emphasized portions: *no deduction . . . in any case . . .* [for] *items specified . . . shall be allowed*. This cuts across all types of income tax returns: individual, corporation, partnership, trust, etc. Yet, you know, we know, and the IRS knows, that on Forms 1120 and 1120S, personal and family expenditures on behalf of the principal owners can be disguised on the corporate books to appear as legitimate business expenses. These are the kinds of things the IRS scrutinizes when it examines the books and records of small business corporations.

In this chapter, therefore, we want to excise from Sections 261 through 280H those particular items which are directed at personal and family expenditures (as distinguishable from bona fide business expenses). There are about seven such sections. The implication is that concerted effort must be expended to separate personal from business matters on the corporation's books. In support of this "concerted effort" requirement, we'll cite pertinent court rulings therewith.

Starting at the Top

In a small C or S corporation, which persons are most likely to foist into the expense and disbursements process, expenditures for personal and family matters?

Answer: The top brass — the principal owners — those officers and directors who, together, control more than 50% of the stock value of the company. Typically, there are five or fewer such persons. Hence, the commingling of personal and business matters seldom trickles down to the minority shareholders or to nonshareholder employees.

Recognizing this fact of life in small business enterprises, Section 262 starts right off prohibiting any commingling of personal and business matters. The section is titled: *Personal, Living, and Family Expenses.* Its subsection (a): *General Rule*, reads as—

Except as otherwise expressly provided in this chapter [of the IR Code], *no deduction shall be allowed for personal, living, or family expenses.*

As the exception clause inplies, deductions from gross income are a matter of legislative grace. For corporations (large or small), the only deductible expenses are those which are "ordinary and necessary" in carrying on a trade or business, or in connection with income-producing property (such as rental property). The term "business expenses" are those incurred in producing, or in the expectation of producing, revenues to the business. Said expenses are distinguished from those expenses incurred for the convenience, comfort, or economy of the individual owners of the business.

Personal and family expenses in connection with a business, the deduction of which is expressly prohibited, include the following: rent paid on property used for residential purposes; life insurance premiums and premiums for insurance on one's residence; cost of maintaining autos and horses for personal use; allowances to minor children; amounts paid as damages in breach of promise suits; attorney fees and legal expenses incurred in connection with personal matters; general household expenses; and others. Personal expenses are nondeductible, regardless of whether they are ordinary and necessary. The "ordinary and necessary" requirement is a test for business expenses only.

When Business Purpose Not Shown

When there is a mixture of personal and business expenses, the burden is on the expense claimant to establish the business purpose of each expense item before any business deduction is allowed. This has been the stance of the IRS and the Tax Court going back as far as 1954. At that time, Section 162: *Trade or Business Expenses*, was enacted. Its subsection (a) then — and now — is:

There shall be allowed as a deduction all the ordinary and necessary expenses paid or incurred during the taxable year in carrying on any trade or business . . .

As an editorial note, let us clarify the distinction between Section 162 and Section 262. Because of the identicalness of the last two digits, there tends to be confusion between these two sections. Section *One* 62 pertains to deductions for business expenses; Section *Two* 62 pertains to the nondeductibility of personal expenses, whether or not associated with a business. With this distinction in mind, let us cite selected court cases that provide instructional guidance for separating personal and business matters.

One case directly on point is that of *J. Dilts*, DC Wyo., 94-1 USTC ¶ 50,162; 845 F Supp 1505. Jerry Dilts and his wife, Barbara Dilts, were the President and Secretary/Treasurer of the Bridle Bit Ranch Company ("Bridle Bit"), an S corporation. They lived in a home owned by the corporation which operated a cattle and sheep ranch in Wyoming. Although there was no written requirement by the corporation that they live on the ranch, the Dilts argued that it was a condition of their employment that they do so. They found that it was necessary to be near the livestock to remove them from railroad tracks and roads, to check on heifers during calving season, to keep an eye on fires that frequently occur on the land, to safeguard ranch equipment and supplies, and to deal with hunters during hunting season.

The expenses at tax issue included home heating costs, groceries for the Dilts and their family, telephone and electricity costs, depreciation of their home, costs of home improvements, satellite dish repairs, and home and automobile insurance premiums.

In its rationale for denying the expenses under Section 262, the court held that—

Everyone must have certain necessities of life, but expenditures to obtain them do not lose their personal characteristics because they may contribute indirectly to a taxpayer's business activities. . . . The taxpayers must demonstrate that the expenses were different from, or in excess of, what would have been spent for personal purposes . . . such that they, as prescribed by the company . . . took on the color of a business expense.

The Dilts failed to show that their expenses were either in excess of what they would have ordinarily incurred or that their expenses lost their personal character. Thus, the Court concluded that the expenses at issue were predominantly personal.

Another case, that of *M.D. Houston*, 47 TCM 83, Dec. 40,544(M), TC Memo 1983-635, relates to an insurance agency business. Here the Court concluded that Houston and his wife could not deduct—

> Losses for truck and auto expenses, disability insurance premiums paid, the cost of flowers worn by the wife at charitable functions, post office box rental expense, the cost of magazine subscriptions, fees for children's school activities, payments for musical equipment used at home, the cost of laundering, telephone services, and boat insurance.

In the case of *J.J. Chambers*, 73 TCM 2766, Dec. 52,043(M), TC Memo 1997-224, who was running a day care center, the Court concluded that—

> Expenditures for groceries, utilities, travel, meals, entertainment, supplies, interest, legal advice, video rentals, and various capital improvements were not deductible as business expenses even though a de minimis amount, order of 5%, could be shown as business related.

We summarize in Figure 10.1 the principles involved in the cited cases. Actually, there is just one principle at stake. Either establish a business purpose and relationship by a preponderance of information, or face all commingled expenses being summarily disallowed as personal and family expenses.

Life Insurance Premiums

It is well recognized that premiums paid by a taxpayer on his own life constitute personal expenses which are nondeductible. Because these expenses are not deductible, the proceeds from a life insurance contract are not taxable This is the significance of Section 101: *Certain Death Benefits.* Its subsection (a)(1) states—

> *Except as otherwise provided . . . gross income **does not include** amounts received (whether in a single sum or*

otherwise) under a life insurance contract, if such amounts are paid by reason of death of the insured. [Emphasis added.]

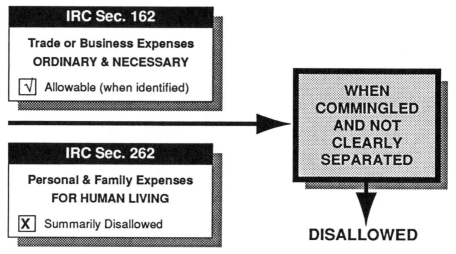

Fig. 10.1 - Distinction Between Sec. 162 & 262: Importance of Separation

For corporations, Section 101(a) opens up a floodgate of ingenious tax-free insurance arrangements for key persons. A "key person" is any officer in, or any 20% owner of, the corporation. For each of these persons, million dollar ($1,000,000) and up policies are purchased by the corporation. In many cases, the corporation borrows the money to buy paid-up life insurance which is then integrated into endowment, annuity, and pension contracts. The company then writes off the interest on the borrowings and the premiums on the contracts as an ordinary and necessary business expense (to keep the key persons on board). In some cases, the key persons can borrow against the cash value of the policies and use the money tax free. That is, provided the borrowed amount is paid back (with interest). If it is not, the borrowings become taxable compensation to the key person(s).

All of this is fine, except for Section 264. This 3,000-word section is titled: *Certain Amounts Paid in Connection with Insurance Contracts.* Its subsection (a) sets the tone by saying—

No deduction shall be allowed for—

> *(1) Premiums on any life insurance policy, or endowment or annuity contract, if the taxpayer is directly or indirectly a beneficiary under the policy or contract.*
>
> *(2) Any amount paid or accrued on indebtedness incurred or continued to purchase or carry a single premium life insurance, endowment, or annuity contract.*

If you read the word "taxpayer" as a C or S corporation, instead of an individual, you will comprehend the focus of Section 264 better. Beginning in tax years ending after June 8, 1997, no deduction is allowed for interest paid or accrued on indebtedness with respect to any life insurance policy or annuity contract covering the life of *any* individual (not just officers, employees, or financially interested individuals), in whom the corporation has an insurable interest. Speculating in life insurance contracts is not the role of an ordinary trade or business.

Using the Corporation as Intermediary

The key persons of a small corporation often use the corporate entity as their own private intermediary for arranging the sales and exchanges of property. They and their family members do this with the intent of creating losses and expenses to the corporation. In the process, they acquire property from the corporation below its true market value, which they intend to subsequently sell for significant gain. In the meantime, the losses and expenses are taken by the corporation. For C corporations, this reduces the taxable income (and therefore reduces the tax). For S corporations, the distributable income is reduced, which in turn helps to reduce the taxable income of each distributee stockholder.

These kinds of "prearranged transactions" between stockholders and their controlled corporation are a No-No. Why?

Because Section 267 makes it so. This section is titled: *Losses, Expenses, and Interest with Respect to Transactions Between Related Taxpayers*. A "related taxpayer" is a key person and members of his family (whether the family members are stockholders or not in the corporation). A related taxpayer situation also exists between a key person and a corporation, whereby with stockholder family members, the key person controls more than 50% of the corporation.

The essence of the 2,800-word Section 267 is its subsection (a)(1): *Deduction for Loss Disallowed*, which reads—

> *No deduction shall be allowed in respect of any loss from the sale or exchange of property, directly or indirectly, between [related] persons. The preceding sentence shall not apply to any loss of the distributing corporation (or the distributee) in the case of a distribution in complete liquidation.*

In other words, except in the case of total dissolution (liquidation) of a corporation, no property losses are attributable to the corporation for dealings with its own stockholders who, directly or indirectly, control more than 50% of the corporation. Furthermore, as per subsection (a)(2): *Matching of . . . Expenses and Interest*, the corporation is not allowed to deduct related expenses or interest, unless the payee stockholder **includes as income** the exact matching amount which the corporation deducts.

Two (among many) court cases on point support the prohibition of Section 267. In *Drake, Inc.*, CA-10, 44-2 USTC ¶ 9503, 145 F2d 365, the Court disallowed a loss from the sale of land by the corporation to one of its stockholders who, through his family, owned more than 50% of the corporation. In *Grady Leasing Corp.*, 74 TCM 541, Dec. 52,238(M), TC Memo 1997-405, the Court would not allow the corporation to deduct a loss arising from the sale of a motor home to its president and sole owner of the corporation.

Company Sponsored Entertainment, Etc.

It is common practice among corporations large and small to sponsor various forms of entertainment, amusement, and recreation to promote their business. Under the promotional umbrella of acquiring new clients and customers, the sponsored activities can sometimes become lavish and extravagant. Nevertheless, the company picks up the tabs and totals them for the year as *Other deductions* on Forms 1120 and 1120S. Because such expenses have both business and personal components, it is often difficult to separate the two. It is for this reason that Section 274 becomes applicable.

Section 274 is titled: *Disallowance of Certain Entertainment, Etc., Expenses.* Its subsection (a)(1), general rule, reads—

> *No deduction otherwise allowable . . . shall be allowed—*
> *With respect to an activity which is of the type generally considered to constitute entertainment, amusement or recreation, UNLESS the taxpayer* [corporation] *establishes that the item was **directly related to**, or, in the case of an item directly preceding or following **a substantial** and bona fide business discussion (including business meetings at a convention or otherwise), that such item **was associated with**, the **active conduct** of the* [corporation's] *trade or business . . . or with respect to a facility* [owned or rented by the corporation] *used in connection with an activity* [above]. [Emphasis added.]

The term "otherwise allowable" is addressed by subsection (d): *Substantiation Required.* The essence here is that—

> *No deduction or credit shall be allowed* [as a bona fide trade or business expense] *unless the* [corporation] *substantiates by adequate records or by **sufficient evidence corroborating** the* [corporation's] *own statement (A) the **amount** of such expense or other item, (B) the **time and place** [*involved*], (C) the **business purpose** of the expense or other item, and (D) the **business relationship** to the* [corporation] *of persons entertained, using the facility or property, or receiving the gift.* [Emphasis added.]

Approximately 34,000 — yes, 34 *thousand* — words of regulations support Section 274! Obviously, the best we can do here is to highlight some of its features in our Figure 10.2. The legislative intent of Section 274 is to deter the indiscriminate claims of entertainment expenses, without corroborating evidence of a clear business purpose thereto.

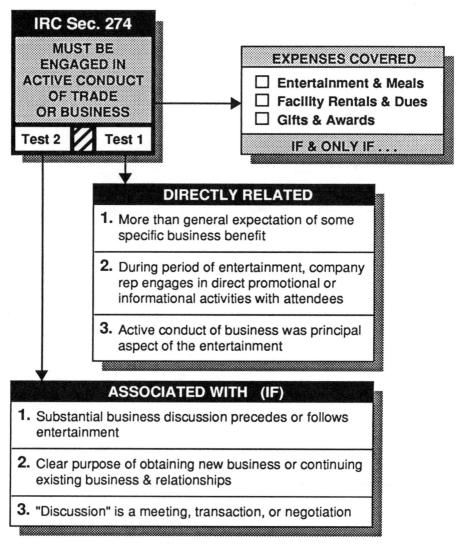

Fig. 10.2 - Key features for Deductibility of Entertainment, Etc. Expenses

The case of *Foster Trenching Co., Inc.,* D.A., Ct Cls, 73-1 USTC ¶ 9235, 473 F2d 1398, brings out an instructive point. It illustrates why no deduction is allowed when a company representative is not present at a company-sponsored entertainment event. The Foster company rented a fishing boat for use by the employees of its best customers. The Foster company paid all the costs of operating the boat, the renting of fishing gear and foul weather clothing, the furnishing of meals and beverages, and made all arrangements for sleeping accommodations (company paid). But no Foster company representative was aboard. The Court held that without such a representative, there was no creation of good will, no advertising advantage, no display of products or services, and no opportunity to initiate a useful business discussion.

Example: Clear Business Purpose

In another instructive case, that of *R.G. Moore, Inc.*, DC Va, 96-2 USTC ¶ 50,413, the validity of extensive entertainment expenses was upheld. The Moores were a husband and wife C corporation in the business of real estate development and building residential homes in new subdivisions. Their gross sales for the tax year at issue (1989) were $57,900,000 (57.9 million).

For a number of years during the 1980s, the Moores hosted an annual party in December. As was their custom, they invited only those real estate agents who had sold at least two of their homes during the year. The party took place in the grand ballroom of a prestigious beachfront hotel in Norfolk, Virginia. The party included a cocktail hour, a seated dinner, dancing, and live entertainment by nationally known professionals (singers, comedians, and musicians).

About midway into the party, Mr. Moore addressed the attendees to thank them for selling his homes during the current year. With posters and slides, he explained his building and subdivision program for the upcoming year, and solicited the continued sales effort of those present and their associates. After his address, he engaged in one-on-one conversations regarding his plans and progress.

The party expenses totaled $347,000. The Moores wrote the entire amount off as entertainment expenses, pursuant to Code Section 274. The IRS disallowed the deduction on Form 1120 because of "distractions" from the business purpose of the party by the professional entertainers. The Court overruled the IRS and allowed the entertainment expense deduction in full.

The Court noted that only those real estate agents who had sold at least two of the Moores' homes during the year were invited to the party. There appeared to be no other motivation in doing so than to promote the sale of new homes in the following year The Court cited Treas. Reg. § 1.274-2(c)(4) re a "clear business setting" by which any recipient of the entertainment would have reasonably known that the Moores' expenditure was directly intended to further the business. Several real estate agents who had attended the party testified on this point. Otherwise, there appeared to be no meaningful personal or social relationship between the Moores and the recipients of the entertainment. Therefore, the Court concluded that the Moores' motive was clearly to advertise and promote the sale of their subdivision-developed homes.

In more specific terms, the Court said:

Given the dramatic effect which the annual parties had on the Moores' business, this Court does not find it difficult to believe that the entertainment aspect of the 1989 party was clearly subordinate to the business purpose of promoting the sale of homes [page 85,377 of 96-2 USTC ¶ 50,413].

Executive Travel Expenses

For nonexecutive and nonkey persons of a corporation, the travel expenses regulations for Sections 162 and 274 are adhered to quite closely. Most managers make sure that their employees "toe the line" with respect to justifying each proposed business trip and in providing substantiating records when seeking reimbursement from the company. It is the executives and key persons of small, closely held corporations who ignore — sometimes flagrantly — the IRS regulations concerning travel. Their attitude seems to be: "Where I travel when, and what I do, is **my** business: not the IRS's business." With classical CEO arrogance and swagger, they instruct their underlings to write off all of their travel expenses (including expenses for their spouses and dependents) against the corporation. Accounting subordinates dare not ask about the justifying details.

Back as far as 1915, the Board of Tax Appeals (BTA), forerunner of the present-day Tax Court, held that—

> The mere authorization of reimbursement to officer-stockholders for costs of travel and entertainment . . . is not sufficient to establish deductibility by the corporation [*Golding & Hahn Co., Inc.*, 15 BTA 499, Dec. 4882].

A few years later (in 1937), the Tax Court (TC) held similarly, to wit—

> If a corporation pays and deducts the travel expenses of an officer-stockholder and the travel is found to be personal in nature, as opposed to business-related, the corporation is denied a deduction for the expenses, and the officer-stockholder realizes taxable income, as a constructive dividend, in the amount of the disallowed expenses. The corporation cannot deduct the disallowed expenses as compensation. [*Challenge Mfg. Co.*, 37 TC 650, Dec. 25,304].

Hence, the position of Congress, the courts, and the IRS has always been that whether the traveler is an officer or a 20% or more owner of the corporation or not, the executives must comply with the same tax regulations as any other employee of the company. There are some differences, however. Executives, by virtue of their position in the company, may be allowed a more comfortable style of travel and lodging, such as going first class. The term "first class" is generally understood to mean those amenities which are top quality without being lavish or extravagant.

Travel and lodging expenses are categorized as: (A) Domestic travel, (B) Foreign travel, and (C) Spousal and dependent travel. All travel includes both business and personal elements. It is important, therefore, that the *primary motivation* for the travel be established. The amount of time during the trip spent on personal activity compared to the amount of time spent on activities directly relating to the corporation's business is a major factor in determining whether the trip was primarily business or personal. Other factors taken in account for the business aspects of travel are presented in Figure 10.3.

The key distinction between domestic and foreign travel is the allocation of costs to and from the business destination. If the

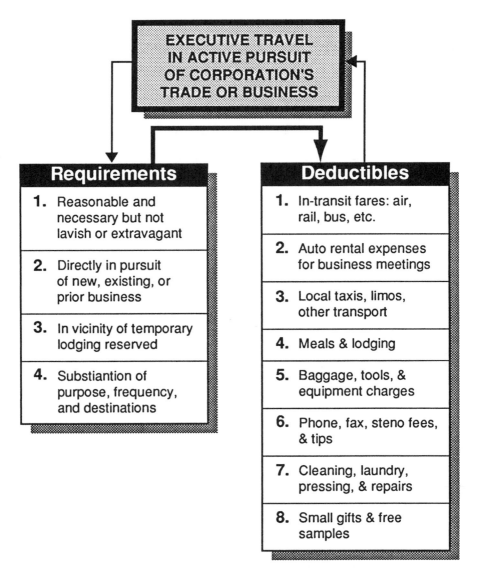

Fig. 10.3 - Deductible Travel Expenses When Reasonable & Necessary

primary purpose is domestic business (determined on an 8-hour workday), all destination and return costs are deductible. As to foreign travel, if the trip is less than one week (seven consecutive days) and one or more bona fide business contacts are made, all destination and return costs are deductible. If the foreign trip is one week or more, and 25% or more is spent on nonbusiness activities, the destination and return costs have to be allocated proportionally.

As to executive travel with spouses, dependents, and others, subsection **274(m)(3)** sets forth specific conditions before any deductions are allowed. This subsection: *Travel Expenses of spouse, dependent, or others*, reads in pertinent part—

No deduction shall be allowed . . . for travel expenses paid or incurred with respect to a spouse, dependent, or other individual accompanying . . . an officer or employee of the [corporation] *on business travel, unless—*

- *(A) the spouse, dependent, or other individual is an employee of the* [corporation],
- *(B) the travel of the spouse, dependent or other individual is for a bona fide business purpose, and*
- *(C) such expenses would otherwise be deductible by the spouse, dependent, or other individual* [as if each were traveling alone]. [Emphasis added.]

Luxury Autos, Boats, Planes

The concept of "executive travel" implies the privilege of unrestricted use of company-owned luxury autos, boats, and planes. The vehicles are purchased in the name of the company and assigned to the controlling officers and shareholders for their personal and business use. All operating expenses are billed to and paid by the corporation. The rationale for doing so is that each assigned executive is on call for business 24 hours a day. This rationale follows from the tax theory of: *For convenience of the employer and as a condition of employment.* This rationale favoring an officer-stockholder does not always pass muster under IRC Section 280F: *Limitation on Depreciation for Luxury Automobiles; Limitation Where Certain Property Used for Personal Purposes.*

Section 280F is a complex body of tax law. We want to point out only those features of it that affect corporate executives. For such purposes, an "executive" is defined as a 5% *owner* of the corporation, whether an officer, director, employee, or other person.

One significant feature of 280F is the term "qualified business use." This generally means that 50% or more of the time that a vehicle or facility is used, it is used directly in the trade or business of the corporation. When the business use is less than 50% stringent disallowance and recapture rules are triggered. There is an exception for private aircraft owned or leased by the corporation. If at least 25% of the aircraft's flight time is for business purposes, the aircraft's use is considered qualified business use [Subsec. 280F(d)(6)(C)(ii)].

A second significant feature of 280F is the term "listed property." This term is defined in subsection 280F(d)(4)(A) as including any—

(1) passenger auto or other property used as a means of transportation;

(2) property generally used for purposes of entertainment, recreation, or amusement; or

(3) computers, cellulars, telecoms, and related peripherals.

The term "other property used as a means of transportation" includes trucks, buses, trains, boats, airplanes, motorcycles, and any other form of vehicle that can be used for transporting persons, goods, or a combination thereof.

The most significant feature of 280F relates to the term "use by 5% owners and related persons." This is the caption of subsection 280F(d)(6)(C)(i) whose essence is—

*The term "qualified business use" **shall not include**—*

(1) leasing property to any 5% owner or related party,

(2) use of property provided as compensation for the performance of service by a 5% owner or related party, or

*(3) use of property provided as compensation for the performance of services by any person not described in subclause (2) **unless an amount is included in the***

gross income of such person with respect to such use, and, where required, there was [income, social security, and medicare tax] *withholdings.* [Emphasis added.]

The clause "unless an amount is included in gross income" is the **right of usage** by corporate executives. How does this work? We'll explain.

Personal Use Affidavits

For those corporate officials who have elite duties to perform, the practice is to provide each such person with a company-owned or leased vehicle, facility, or item of equipment. The type and value of the vehicle or facility assigned to each executive is in keeping with his/her corporate status. The assignee has 100% use of the item. This means that it can be used for personal purposes as well as for business purposes. The only requirement is that the executive provide to the corporation a statement or affidavit as to the estimated percentage of personal use of the item throughout the year. Typically, this personal use percentage is in the neighborhood of 25%. Sometimes it is another amount but always less than 50%.

The authorization and procedures for personal use affidavits must be set forth in the official bylaws of the corporation. This requires the notice of a Directors' meeting, a resolution, its adoption, and a recording in the Minutes Book. Recall our discussions in Chapter 1: Corporate Bona Fides. Once the personal use affidavit becomes the approved policy of the company, standardized affidavit forms can be printed on company letterhead. Each executive to whom a vehicle, facility, or item of equipment is assigned, is expected to fill in and complete one affidavit form each year. The executive's signature certifies that the personal use amount shown is true and correct as to his/her best belief and estimate. No verification or intrusive questions are asked.

The accounting department keeps track of all operating expenses on each executive vehicle or facility. Once each month, the personal use percentage of each executive is applied to the company paid amounts. The results then go to the payroll department for inclusion in the executive's gross income.

For example, suppose an executive was furnished with an $85,000 mid-stretch limousine. The total operating costs paid by the company (lease payments, insurance, gasoline, chauffeur, security, accessories, maintenance, etc.) came to $12,680 for the month under consideration. The personal use affidavit by the executive showed 25%. The amount included in that executive's gross income for that month would be:

$12,680 x 0.25 = $3,170.

It might be a higher or lower amount of inclusion the next month.

What happens if the executive's actual personal use was 65% instead of 25%? Who is likely to assert the 65%? Certainly, no subordinate. Nor would any other executive of the same company (who may also be using his assigned vehicle more than 25% for personal use).

The only challenger would be the IRS. Suppose, for example, that an IRS examiner, after looking over distance and destination records on the vehicle, concludes that 55% was personal use. What would happen?

Most likely, the company accountant would concede to the IRS. He would not want to cause any problem for the executive or for the corporation. He would offer to include as "other income" to the corporation the amount of

$12,680 x (0.55 − 0.25) = $12,680 x 0.30 = $3,805.

Such an arrangement, when accepted, becomes a mutually agreed *audit adjustment*. Once accomplished, no one else need ever know. Not the executive . . . nor any stockholder of the corporation.

11

BASIS IN STOCK HELD

The Term "Basis" Is The Amount Of Capital (Money) Or Money Equivalent Invested In Stock. In a Close Corporation, Self-Dealings Between Controlling Shareholders And The Corporation, And Between The Shareholders Themselves, Promote INADEQUATE Basis Records. This Follows From The "Acquisition Character" Of The Stock Which May Be: (1) Founder, (2) Strike, (3) FMV, (4) Dividend, (5) Gift, Or (6) Inherited. Each Stock Character Has A Separate Tax Basis Of Its Own. Therefore, Each Shareholder Must Track Independently His Basis In The Event His Stock Is Someday Sold Or Exchanged.

There are three types of stockholders in a small C or S corporation. These are: (1) the founders, (2) the principals, and (3) the investors. All three types contribute money and/or property to the corporation with the expectation that they may sell or exchange their stock someday . . . at a gain. Whether they do so at a gain or at a loss depends on their individual self-discipline in keeping track of their tax basis in the stock that they hold. Because we are dealing with privately-held stock and the private transactions thereof, there is no common broker or intermediary to do the recordkeeping and basis adjustments that are necessary. Consequently, for reasons which will be more apparent later, the founders, principals, and investors all will have a different tax basis in each share of stock that each owns. Posting and tracking said basis is the responsibility of each individual shareholder.

The founders are the originators and formulators of the corporation. They provide a limited amount of "seed money" to do the incorporation, organize its management team and bylaws, and oversee the startup and initial operation of the entity. Once the operation is underway, the founders take on a more passive role as directors.

The principals, on the other hand, are the ongoing officers and managers of the corporation. They are active daily participants who keep the company rolling on an upward path of increasing gross receipts and improved net earnings. They hire employees, seek investors, and arrange for lines of credit to meet the cash shortfalls as needed.

What we want to do in this chapter, therefore, is to review (rather quickly) the fundamentals of basis accounting for each share of stock in the company. This necessitates the describing of the basis differences between founders' shares, purchasing of shares, exchanging property and services for shares, gifted shares, and inherited shares. We also want to point out some of the "adjustments to basis" required when dividends and nontaxable distributions are declared.

Shareholders Ledger Not Relevant

Back in Chapter 1: Corporation Bona Fides, we discussed the importance of a shareholders ledger. We presented Figure 1.3 (on page 1-11) which listed the contents of this ledger. Its primary purpose is fulfillment of the corporation's legal obligation to keep track of its shareholders (names, addresses, Tax IDs), the number of shares held by each shareholder, and the voting rights of said shares. The ledger serves more as a control function than as an accounting function. There is no obligation by the corporation to track each stockholder's individual tax basis in the stock that each shareholder owns.

As long as a shareholder contributes only money to the corporation, the ledger record of the dollars received for the number of shares issued can be considered a contributor's *initial basis* in his stock held. But if one contributes property or services instead of money, the shareholders ledger bears no relevance to that contributor's tax basis in the stock he acquires. Let us illustrate with an example.

Suppose a shareholder contributes a small commercial building to the corporation for use as its home office and initial operations. Suppose the building has a fair market value (FMV) of $200,000 as professionally appraised. Assume an issue price of $100 per share. Thus, in exchange for the $200,000 FMV building, the contributor would receive 2,000 shares of stock (2,000 sh x $100/sh = $200,000). What is the contributor's tax basis in the stock? *Hint*: It is NOT $100/sh.

Answer: It depends. Suppose the contributor purchased the building outright for $135,000. Since it was a commercial building, he either used it for his own business or he rented it to some other small business. Depending on the length of time of business use, he would be allowed a certain amount of depreciation on the building as capital cost recovery. Suppose he had taken $65,000 in allowable depreciation. His tax basis in the building is now $70,000 (135,000 – 65,000), called: *adjusted basis*. In other words, the contributor's basis in the $200,000 FMV building exchanged with the corporation for 2,000 shares of stock would be $35 per share ($70,000 basis ÷ 2,000 sh).

The overall net effect is that the corporation carries on its books a $200,000 FMV building which becomes **its** initial basis for depreciation purposes. Simultaneously, the contributor carries on his books 2,000 shares of stock at $35 per share. So important is this corporation-contributor basis-difference concept that we present a depiction of it in Figure 11.1. The message intended is that it is incumbent upon each shareholder to keep adequate books and records of his tax basis on all close corporation shares that he holds.

Contributions to Capital

Any corporation can accept money as a contribution to capital, in exchange for its stock. When it does so, the capital received is NOT included in the gross income of the corporation. Instead, the amount received becomes part of its assets; the stock issued becomes part of its liabilities (as stockholder equity).

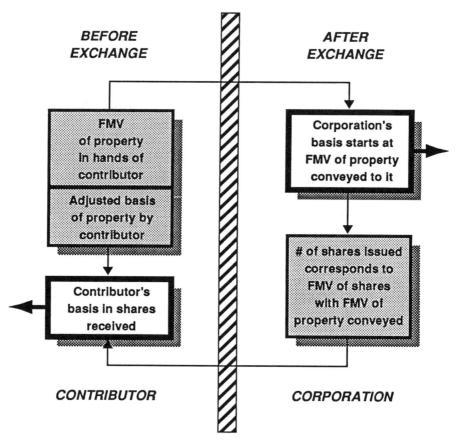

Fig. 11.1 - Basis Differences When Exchanging Property for Stock

This is a *balance sheet* matter: not an income and expense matter. Such is the impact of IRC Section 118: ***Contributions to the Capital of a Corporation.*** Its subsection (a) reads—

> *In the case of a corporation, gross income does not include **any contribution** to* [its] *capital.* [Emphasis added.]

Note the emphasized term "any contribution." There are three types of said contributions: money, property, and service. Money is direct capital; property has a capital equivalency; and services are a conversion to capital. Ordinarily, most nonexecutive employees contribute money, as do most outside investors. Their tax basis in the shares acquired is the amount of money contributed divided by the number of shares they receive. It is the founders and the principals of the corporation who seek to contribute property and services in lieu of money. This creates — or can create — serious basis problems.

Contributed property may be in the form of real estate (land, buildings, commercial structures), tangible items (vehicles, equipment, machinery), and/or intangible items (a founder's prior business name, unsecured promissory notes, stock in some other company acquired by gift or inheritance). The "capital equivalency" issue is: Is the property readily convertible to money? And, if so, what is its fair market value? Is the FMV assigned to it by a founding contributor or by a principal contributor true and correct? Most probably not. And herein lies the basis problem.

Let us assume that the by-laws of the corporation authorize the acceptance of property in exchange for its shares. Can you not sense the valuation abusiveness when a founder or a principal contributes his/her own property to the corporation?

There are two such possibilities. One possibility — likelihood(?) — is that property that can be used by the corporation is *overvalued* at time of the exchange. The second possibility is that property which has absolutely no use to the corporation — therefore *worthless* — will be forced upon the corporation by one or more of the controlling interests. Let us exemplify both possibilities.

Example 1: Consider that there is a rundown old commercial building which, after extensive repairs and renovation, the corporation could use. One of the principals owns the building and offers it in exchange for stock. The building, if it were professionally appraised at the time of the offer would FMV at $13,000. However, the contributor insists that its exchange-for-stock value is $33,000. In other words, he wants $20,000 more in stock than the property would sell for on the open market. Who is going to challenge the contributor in this case? Isn't this an abuse of executive power?

Example 2: Consider that one of the founders has an unsecured promissory note for $100,000 and 1,000 shares of some obscure corporation which he inherited from his great aunt. He wants to foist both items onto the corporation for $20,000 in stock. Both items are worthless to the corporation. Neither item has any true market value. Still, the contributor insists. Isn't this also an abuse of executive power?

The possible abuses above, and others similar, should be addressed head-on in the bylaws of the corporation. Instead of merely authorizing the acceptance of property in exchange for its stock, there should be a requirement that the offer be accompanied by an *independent* professional appraisal as to the FMV of the property. Additionally, the bylaws should make it clear that, unless the offered property can be put to immediate use in the business operations, it will not be accepted. The corporation is not a repository for rundown, damaged, and worthless items pawned off on it by the controlling interests.

When Services Exchanged

Personal services rendered to the corporation can also be exchanged for stock in the corporation. But guess whose personal services would be acceptable? Answer: Those serving as founders, directors, officers, and managers . . . obviously! Here is where executive abuse can show up again.

The tax law on a service-for-stock exchange is addressed by IRC Section 83: *Property Transferred in Connection with Performance of Services*. Its subsection (a) reads in pertinent part—

If, in connection with the performance of services, property is transferred to any person . . ., the excess of—

(1) the fair market value of such property . . . at the first time the rights of the person having the beneficial interest in such property are transferable . . ., over (2) the amount (if any) paid for such property, shall be included in the gross income of the persons who performed such services . . . . [Emphasis added.]

The term "property" includes any item of value other than money.

The clause: "at the first time the rights . . . are transferable" implies two things. One implication is that the stock can be issued in the name of a family member or "any person," other than he who actually performs the services. This feature derives from the opening clause: *If, in connection with the performance of services.* The second implication is that restrictions can be put on the stock until the service performer complies with all terms of the contractual arrangements as spelled out in the company bylaws.

There is a clear requirement in Section 83(a) that whoever performs the services for stock MUST INCLUDE the FMV of the stock in his gross income. This means the issuance of a Form W-2: *Wage and Tax Statement*, with all of its required withholdings. As depicted in Figure 11.2, we suggest a separate W-2 of its own. This becomes the recipient's *basis-in-stock* document, should the IRS make inquiry into any self-dealing arrangements among the controlling interests of the corporation.

When issuing a W-2 in exchange for stock, an interesting dilemma is raised. As restricted stock, it cannot be sold (for money) at the time of its transfer. Therefore, should the number of shares of stock be issued for the gross FMV included in income, or for the net take-home after withholdings?

The answer is: Either way. If the stock is issued for the gross FMV, the service performer has to pay all of the tax withholdings out of his own pocket. Only then is his basis (after tax) the same as the gross FMV. If the number of shares is issued for the net take-home amount, no additional tax need be paid. Let us illustrate.

Assume that $20,000 of bona fide services were performed in exchange for stock. Assume that the stock is par valued at $100 per share. Also assume that all federal and state tax withholdings amount to $8,000. This means a net take-home of $12,000 (20,000 − 8,000). Should the company issue 200 shares ($20,000 ÷ $100/sh) or 120 shares ($12,000 ÷ $100/sh)? The recipient's basis in each share is the same: $100 per share. The difference is that for the 200 shares the service performer has to come up with $8,000 out of his own pocket (and pay it to the company). The net effect is that he will have bought an additional 80 shares (200 − 120) on his own. This is the significance of the catchy wording in Section 83(a) that—

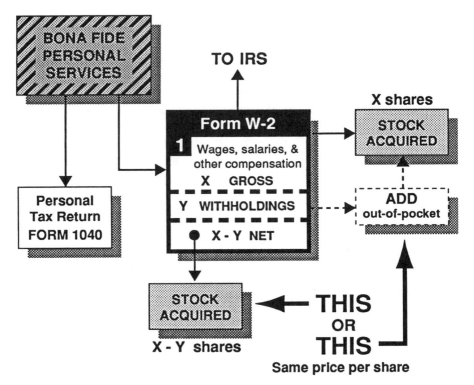

Fig. 11.2 - Dilemna Posed When Personal Services Exchanged for Stock

If . . . the excess of . . . the [FMV] *of such property . . . over the amount (if any) paid . . .* [is] *included in the gross income of the person who performed* [the] *services.*

The fundamental requirement in Section 83(a) is this: There is no escaping one's tax obligations (income tax, social security tax, medicare tax, etc.) when performing services in exchange for stock. Except for founder shares (which we'll discuss below), there is no free stock that the company can issue. Every share of stock must have a documentable tax basis, even if that basis is zero.

Founder Shares: Basis In

The nearest thing to free stock in small C or S corporations is the issuance of founder shares. These are issued at a very low par value (such as 10 cents per share) primarily for recordkeeping purposes. Their issuance is an ethereal form of exchange for the experience, expertise (technical, financial, marketing), and business contacts of the corporation's founders. Such persons are the directors and officers of the corporation for its organization, startup, and initial operation.

Serious founders may agree among themselves as to what percentage of the total initial authorized shares shall be founder shares. A reasonable percentage range would be from 5% to 15% of the authorized number of shares. For example, if the authorized initial number of shares were 100,000 shares, and the founders agreed (in the bylaws) that 12% of that number would be issued to themselves, there would be 12,000 founder shares. (100,000 sh x 0.12). This would leave 88,000 nonfounder shares for issue at a strike price other than par value.

The 12,000 shares of founder stock at a par value of 10 cents per share ($0.10/sh) would provide only $1,200 (12,000 sh x $0.10/sh) of capital to the company. This is NOT ENOUGH CAPITAL to get a small C or S corporation up and running. The founders have to do better than this. They have to come up with some real money out of their pockets. They have to set a strike price for the nonfounder shares at somewhere between $10 and $100 per share. The founders themselves have to purchase enough nonfounder shares to cover all organizational and startup costs that can be reasonably anticipated.

For illustration purposes, let us assume that, based on reputable professional estimates, $250,000 is needed for startup and initial operations. If there were five co-founders, for example, each would have to come up with $50,000 on his own: money or property but not services. At a strike price of $50 per share, say, that would be 1,000 nonfounder shares per co-founder. Altogether, then, each co-founder would hold the following shares:

2,400 founder shares at $0.10/sh	= $ 240
[12,000 founder shares ÷ 5 co-founders]	
1,000 nonfounder shares at $50/sh	= 50,000
3,400 shares	$50,240

Each co-founder has the obligation to record and track his own cost basis in the shares he holds. In the illustration above, he can keep — for basis purposes — his founder and nonfounder shares separate. Or, he can combine them into one average cost per share. This is permissible in the startup phase of a corporation before any additional shareholders (as nonfounders) come on the scene.

Using this rationale, the average cost per share in the illustration above would be:

$$\$50,240 \div 3,400 \text{ sh} = \underline{\$14.78/\text{sh}}$$

The $14.78/sh is the initial reference base (tax basis) for determining capital gain or capital loss, at some point in time downstream.

Additional Stock for Cash

In the startup of a business venture, the founders and principals should provide all of the risk capital, initially. Seldom does this happen, but in theory it should. Then, after most of the organizational and operational imperfections have been worked out — say, a year or two after startup — expansion capital will be needed. This is the time for bringing additional shareholders on board. In doing so, be aware that the pool of additional shareholders must come from family members, close friends, and trusted business associates. A private corporation, as you surely must know, cannot solicit shareholders from the public at large.

At a special Board of Directors meeting, a cutoff date should be adopted indicating that, hereafter, all new shareholders shall pay cash. No further exchanges of property or services for stock will be accepted. At this point, the stock has to be issued at a price reflective of the FMV of the corporation. A base estimate of the stock FMV can be made from the latest filed Form 1120/1120S balance sheets. This is called: *book value* . . . or floor value. Such value can be rounded up to reflect the going value of stock in those corporations which offer products and/or services comparable to those of your corporation.

To add professionalism to the FMV process, the bylaws should require that, once each year, the FMV of the company's stock should be appraised and stated for the record. For that year, the FMV price should remain fixed for all coming-on-board shareholders. Each subsequent year, a new FMV would be established. New subscribers then would pay the FMV price corresponding to the year of the stock acquisition.

Whatever is paid in cash for stock, becomes its tax basis. It's that simple. There is also simplicity in the fact that private stock does not change hands as frequently as publicly traded stock. The stockholders, being closely related to one another, understand that their holdings are intended to be long-term rather than short-term. This adds capital stability to any small C or S corporation.

Taxable Stock Dividends

After the first few years of operation, the corporation should be earning profits to some extent. Except for those earnings retained on the books for specific capital needs, dividends should be formally declared. After all, this is the hallmark of a corporation: the sharing of profits among all stockholders, pro rata. As we have pointed out earlier, close corporations tend not to declare dividends, preferring instead to raise officer salaries and/or permit "borrowing" from the accumulated earnings of the corporation. We caution against this practice. The earnings and profits belong to all shareholders, proportionately.

Once declared, the dividends must be paid. The payments can be made in money, stock, or other property. If dividends are paid in stock, it should be at the written request and consent of each shareholder who wishes to participate. Where the need for additional capital is foremost, an incentive sweetener can be added. Such could be a discount comparable to the rate of interest that would have to be paid on a commercial loan at the time of the dividend declaration. For example, if an 8% discount were offered, a dividend-receiving shareholder could acquire stock at 92% of its FMV, established annually as above. As incentive stock, a minimum one-year holding period restriction would apply.

On the subject of dividends, IRC Section 316: *Corporate Distributions; Dividends*, is definitionally relevant. Its subsection (a) says—

*The term "dividend" means any distribution of property made by a corporation to its shareholders . . . **out of its earnings and profits** of the taxable year (computed as of the close of the taxable year without diminution by reason of any distributions made during the taxable year), without regard to the amount of the* [prior years' accumulated] *earnings and profits at the time the distribution was made.* [Emphasis added.]

The point of Section 316(a) is that all dividends paid out of earnings and profits (E & P) are *taxable* to the distributee shareholders. The taxable-to-shareholder amount is determined as of "the close of the [corporation's] taxable year." The total taxable amount to shareholders includes: (1) dividends paid during the year, if any; (2) dividends paid at end of year from current-year E & P, if any; and (3) dividends paid from prior years' accumulated [undistributed] E & P, if any. All dividends are computed pro rata for each shareholder. Whether or not a distributee-shareholder acquires additional stock in the corporation (at a "sweetened" FMV price) is an individual choice. Unlike personal service income, there are no required withholdings on dividends. Furthermore, there is no social security tax, no medicare tax, and no state disability tax on said dividends. These no-tax features alone make dividend stock attractive. As a result, dividend-acquired stock will carry a separate tax basis of its own.

At this point in our discussion, we have the likelihood of four different tax bases in the private stock of a close corporation. These different bases are:

1. Founders basis (as per directors' resolution)
2. Strike basis (before FMV established annually)
3. FMV basis (each year of cash acquisition)
4. Dividend basis (each year of E & P declarations)

Perhaps now you can see the need for basis tracking by each shareholder for the number and issue dates of the stock shares he holds. The longer the company is in operation, and the more successful it becomes, the more difficult it is to "remember" one's basis in the stock held. Clearly, some form of disciplined recordkeeping is required. A suggestion in this regard is presented in Figure 11.3. Note that within each different *acquisition-character* of shares, the average dollar per share basis is used.

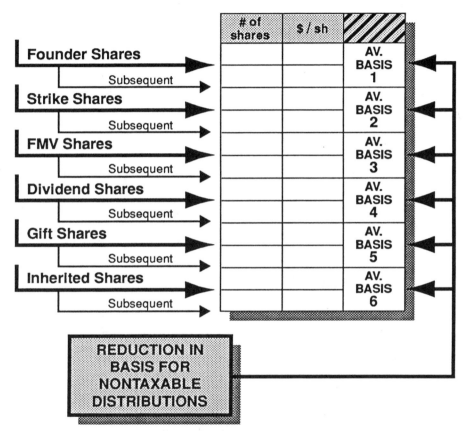

Fig. 11.3 - Disciplined Recordkeeping of Basis Matters in Close Stock

Nontaxable Distributions Reduce Basis

When it becomes evident that the corporation is self-sustaining and reasonably successful, there is a desire on the part of the founders and principals to want some of their capital investment back. Their rationale goes like this: "We loaned money to the corporation to get it going; now, we want some of our money back. We'll declare ourselves a nontaxable distribution. By so doing, we will retain our existing percentage of ownership control." Soon, the self-congratulatory rationale spins out of control. The controlling interests want more and more of their money back, to the point where they have zero investment. But they still want to retain more than 50% control of the business. This is NOT the way things work!

Nontaxable distributions — often misnamed "dividends" — when duly voted upon at a shareholders' meeting, are tax legal. The legality is based on the premise that each $1 per share distribution reduces the tax basis in the stock shares held by a corresponding $1. In other words, a nontaxable distribution is the *return of capital*. It is well known that the return of capital is not taxed. It is less well known that the tax basis in unrelinquished stock MUST BE REDUCED pro rata, by the amount of capital returned. In a closely held corporation, who is going to police the reduction in basis by each individual shareholder? In reality, when nontaxable distributions are formally declared, only the most conscientious shareholders adjust downward their basis records (in Figure 11.3) as they should.

For example, assume that your basis in the stock of your C or S corporation is $26.85 per share. A $10 per share nontaxable distribution is declared. Your adjusted basis ex-distribution is $16.85 per share (26.85 – 10.00). Though your per share tax basis is reduced, you still retain the same number of voting shares.

Now, suppose you were a founder or other principal whose average basis in the stock is $3 per share. The same $10 per share nontaxable distribution as above was declared. What effect does this $10 per share distribution have on the shares that you retain?

Answer: Two effects. The first effect is that you have — or should have — reduced your basis from $3 to $0 (zero) per share. You cannot reduce your basis in stock below zero. Even zero basis stock, if bona fide, retains its voting rights.

The second effect is what happens to that $7 per share (10 – 3) excess distribution. The $7 excess-over-basis becomes a *taxable* distribution. While the corporation may have declared it a nontaxable (return of capital) distribution, the corporation is not required to know or to maintain each shareholder's individual tax basis records. We state again that any excess-over-basis distribution is **taxable!**

It is taxable as ordinary dividends: NOT as capital gain. To get capital gain treatment, you have to redeem your shares — all of them. While capital gain treatment is more tax beneficial than ordinary dividend treatment, redemption of your shares means relinquishment of your voting rights and ownership control of the corporation.

All dividends and distribution declared by a corporation are reported to the IRS on **Form 1099-DIV**: *Dividends and Distributions*. Ordinary dividends are reported in box 1 of said form; nontaxable distributions are reported in box 3. The box 1 corporate reportings are IRS computer matched with whatever each stockholder reports on his own return. The box 3 corporate reportings go unmatched . . . until such time as shares are sold or exchanged and that stockholder's return is IRS selected for audit.

Basis in Gifted Stock

The ownership of a close corporation, whether C or S, tends to be "family and friends" oriented. That is, most stockholders are related taxpayers. The consequence is that, over time, one or more of the shareholders will have acquired their stock by *gift* from other shareholders in the company. When this happens, the basis in said stock is set by Section 1015: *Basis of Property Acquired by Gifts and Transfers in Trust.*

Section 1015(a) states in part that—

*If this property was acquired by gift . . ., the basis **shall be the same** as it would be in the hands of the donor or the last preceding owner by whom it was not acquired by gift. **Except that**, if such basis (adjusted for the period before the date of the gift . . .) is greater than the fair market value of the property at the time of the gift, then for the **purpose of determining loss**, the basis shall be such fair market value . . . .* [Emphasis added.]

This rule is called: "transfer of basis" . . . from donor to donee. There are actually two rules here: a gain rule and a loss rule. The gain rule is that, if the donor's basis is less than the FMV at the time of the gift, the transferred basis is the donor's basis. The loss rule is that, if the donor's basis is more than the FMV (at time of gift), the transferred basis is the FMV. Such is the role of "except that . . ." cited above. We illustrate this distinction for you in Figure 11.4. The idea behind Section 1015(a) is that the donee derives no basis advantage relative to other stockholders in the company.

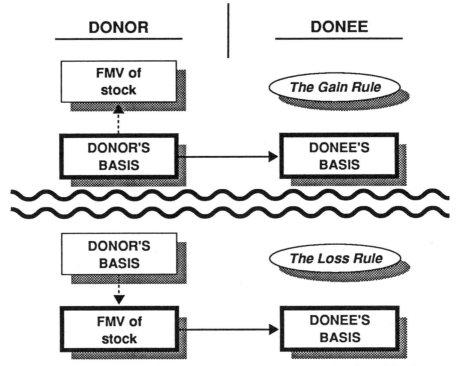

Fig. 11.4 - The Two "Basis Transfer" Rules When Stock Is Gifted

To illustrate this two-rule concept, let us use simple numbers. One of the principals gifts to his son 200 shares of stock whose FMV is $50 per share. Thus, the FMV of the gift is $10,000 (200 sh x $50/sh). The donor's basis is $15 per share (or $3,000). Under the gain rule, the donee's basis is $3,000 in the 200 shares (or $15/sh). The statutory intent here, obviously, is to prohibit the donor from escaping tax on the $7,000 of capital gain (10,000 FMV

– 3,000 basis). If the stock is later sold at a gain relative to the donee's $3,000 basis, the donee — not the donor — pays the tax thereon.

As to the loss rule part of Section 1015(a), suppose the donor's basis (in the illustration above) was $10,000 and the FMV at time of gift was $3,000. In this case, there is a built-in loss of $7,000 (3,000 FMV – 10,000 basis). The donee's basis is $3,000: the *lower* of FMV or basis. If the stock is sold later for $1,000, the donee's loss is $2,000 (3,000 – 1,000); it is NOT $9,000 (2,000 + 7,000). The $7,000 is called a "loss-loss". The donor loses it; the donee loses it. In a case like this, it is better for the donor to sell or exchange the stock to/with an unrelated party, and claim the capital loss on his own return Then, if he wishes to do so, gift the proceeds for a new stock basis start.

Basis in Inherited Stock

When stock is acquired by inheritance (from a decedent) instead of by gift (from a donor), the basis rule is rather simple. The recipient of the stock takes as his basis its FMV at the time of the decedent's death. It is immaterial what the decedent's adjusted basis was, while he was alive. Such is the concept of Section 1014: *Basis of Property Acquired from a Decedent.*

Section 1014 comprises about 1,400$^+$ words of text. The significant portion for us here is its subsection (a). This subsection: *In General*, reads in part as—

The basis of property in the hands of a person acquiring the property from a decedent or to whom the property passed from a decedent shall, if not sold, exchanged, or otherwise disposed of before the decedent's death by such person, be—

(1) the fair market value of the property at the date of the decedent's death . . .

We have cited only 56 words of the total count in Section 1014. The uncited words deal with FMV exceptions under special valuation rules for family farms and businesses, property in trust,

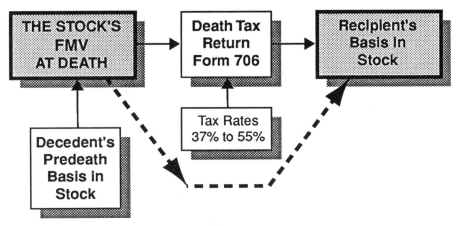

Fig. 11.5 - The "Transfer Taxing" of Stock at Time of Death

annuities, property received by a decedent by gift within one year of his death, and adjustments and exclusions which are beyond our discussion.

There is a bona fide tax rationale for the FMV basis in stock when acquired from a decedent. When a decedent dies, a death tax — called: transfer tax — applies. This is so ordained by Section 2001: *Imposition of Estate Tax*. Its subsection (a) reads—

A tax is hereby imposed on the transfer of the taxable estate of every decedent who is a citizen or resident of the United States.

The rate starts at 37% for taxable estates over $500,000 and extends to 55% for estates over $3,000,000. As depicted in Figure 11.5, any predeath appreciation of unsold stock is **fully taxed** at time of death. The tax applies to the FMV of any stock at that time.

After certain exclusions, the transfer tax is based upon the gross FMV (less allowable deductions) of all property in the decedent's estate at the time of his death. Therefore, if the FMV of a particular item, such as stock, is higher than or lower than the decedent's adjusted basis in that stock, the process of transfer taxing smoothes out the differences. As a consequence, the recipient of the inherited stock starts with an FMV basis as though he had acquired the stock on his own with equivalent after-tax money.

12

SELL, MERGE, OR GO PUBLIC

Usually Within 5 Years, Every Small (Privately-Held) Corporation Faces A Major Decision. If Its Gross Receipts Have Not Reached $2,000,000, Selling The Corporation May Be Indicated. Otherwise, Merging With An Existing Public Corporation Can Be Satisfying. If Truly Exciting Growth Is Sought, "Going Public" May Be Preferred. Registering Stock With The SEC Is Time Consuming, Costly, And DISCLOSURE SENSITIVE. A Respectable Target Goal Of Issuance Is $50,000,000 . . . NET Of Expenses. Said Stock, When Held More Than 5 Years, Qualifies For 10% Capital Gain Tax Treatment Under IRC Sec. 1202(a).

While in theory a corporation has indefinite life, it rarely has indefinite life in its original form. With the passage of time, five to ten years or so, the controlling stockholders begin developing other plans. These "other plans" may include dissolution of the corporation, retiring or buying out some of the principals, selling out to another group of principals, recapitalization and expanding the business, merging with another similar product or service corporation, engaging in a tax-free (stock-for-stock) reorganization with a larger corporation, transferring of assets to an existing public corporation, or going public as a revitalized corporation. These and other options are always open to an entrepreneurially viable undertaking.

In general, it takes at least five years before any business can establish its niche in the marketplace. It simply takes time to generate good will and build a solid reputation behind the product or service being offered to consumers. A good reputation is the position any company should be in, if it wants to attract other owners to it. Indeed, attracting other owners should always be the primary motivation of every small business enterprise.

Attracting other owners, however, becomes a challenge in corporate liquidations (IRC Secs. 331-346), corporate reorganizations (IRC Secs. 351-374), corporate acquisitions (IRC Secs. 381-385), and registration of stock with the Securities and Exchange Commission. This is heavy duty stuff. We estimate that well over 2,000,000 (2 million) words or more of tax and securities laws, regulations, and administrative rulings could be involved. Obviously, all we can do in this (our final) chapter is to touch on the more informative and instructional highlights of selling a corporation, merging with other corporations, or going public on one's own. If "going public" is your target of excitement, be prepared with $1,000,000 ($1 million) or so in cash to surmount the tax, legal, administrative, and competitive hurdles that will be surely in your way.

Preliminary Decisions to Make

Before launching into an all-out effort to attract other owners, step back and reflect on the corporate progress that you have made thus far. For example, ask yourself: "Is our corporation on a clear path of increasing asset value and/or increasing profits? Is our corporation in a position that new owners who are not family and friends would want to become part of, take over, and move on?" You really cannot answer these questions until management has made some preliminary analysis and decisions.

The first decision is whether to dissolve the corporation or to continue on. Dissolution is the formal process of winding down the corporate operations, closing its books, and redeeming all shares outstanding. If, by the fifth taxable year, the corporation has not reached gross receipts in the range of $1,000,000 to $2,000,000, dissolution may be the only practical option. A so-so corporation just isn't going to attract new owner interest.

But, if the gross receipts in the fifth-plus taxable year are in the range of $5,000,000 or more, continuing onward is realistic. Before doing so, if you are an S-status corporation, should you continue as an S or change to a C? This is a second decision to make.

An S corporation, because of its pass-through tax features is attractive for family estates and trusts. Estates for two years after death, qualified subchapter S trusts [subsec. 1361(d)], and electing small business trusts [subsec. 1361(e)] can be shareholders as long as the trustees thereof are U.S. citizens or aliens who are U.S. residents. Estates and trusts of the founders and principals can bring new money into the S entity. But attracting non-family ownership in large numbers would be rare. If you are seeking constructive growth in the company, there is little choice but to convert to a C corporation. This will require a Resolution of Revocation, by which more than 50% of the shareholders must consent [subsec. 1362(d)(1)]. A C corporation, because it is so flexible as to who, where, and what, is more acceptable to nonfamily-related owners than is an S corporation.

A third decision is to appraise the C corporation as it presently stands, and establish pro forma estimates as to its future possibilities. This would require outside consultants to study and compute the gross fair market value of the corporation with respect to *all* of its assets — real, tangible, and intangible — and come up with realistic projections of market growth, new product and service lines, and where the competition is strong and where it is weak. The end product of this effort should be a written report that can be repackaged as an Information Brochure to prospective new owners. This brochure should contain a history of the company, testimonials from well-known customers, a brief description of proprietary items (patents, copyrights, trademarks), and a digest of the latest three years of tax filings. Stamp **every page** of the brochure that it is PRIVATE & CONFIDENTIAL and that it is NOT to be construed as a public solicitation.

A fourth decision is to call a joint special meeting of shareholders and directors to discuss corporate intentions and to appoint an exploratory committee. It should be a three-member committee. Each member should have a special area of expertise of his own, such as: (1) product/service development and production,

(2) sales and marketing, and (3) accounting and finance. Set a budget for this committee. Also set a time frame for producing a written report with recommendations.

Instructions to Committee

The purpose of an exploratory committee is to research and investigate three possible options, namely:

I   — Selling the business
II — Merging with another business
III — Expanding business by going public

No one specific option should be emphasized over others. The idea is to develop enough information and insight to make a sound decision for the next step. The common goal of all options is to enhance the "wealth effect" of the existing shareholders of the corporation.

Encourage the committee to particularly identify the pitfalls of applicable (1) tax laws, (2) securities laws, (3) regulations (federal, state, local), (4) legal requirements, (5) competitive practices, and (6) transitional hurdles from present status to new status. Of course, use the Internet for research as much as is beneficial, but do not overlook print media, law and business libraries, radio and TV, word of mouth, and the placement of subtle exploratory advertising. The goal is to attract serious inquiry by would-be new owners and managers. The goal is NOT to attract or solicit new investors.

Extreme care must be taken by the committee to assure that its exploratory efforts are not construed as a public offering of stock shares. Among the precautionary steps to take are:

Step 1.   Forbid the issuance of any stock to a new person during the exploratory period. Any new person could be a legal, securities, or competitor informant.

Step 2.   Have every response to a serious inquiry reviewed by a legal person knowledgeable in contract and securities law. This is to minimize accusations of a public offering.

Step 3.   Before any and every meeting with a prospective buyer, mergerer, or underwriter (for public offering), submit a preprinted document for signaturizing that: (a) all information conveyed will be held in confidence; (b) the event is not a solicitation for sale of stock; and (c) both sides acknowledge that the exploring company holds private, unregistered stock only.

A general summary of what we have presented thus far is depicted in Figure 12.1. Because this is a tax book, from this point on we'll address mostly the tax aspects of any transitional decision ultimately made. Legal and securities matters, while transitionally dominant, are not the day-to-day operating and tax concerns of most shareholders.

Effect of Sale on Shareholders

Selling a private (small business) corporation is quite unlike that of selling stock in a publicly-traded corporation. No securities-type broker is involved. Instead, the services of real estate brokers, business consultants, liquidating agents, and attorneys knowledgeable in bulk sales contracts are required. This is because you are not selling individual shares of stock; you are selling a *basket of assets*: real, tangible, and intangible. The "basket" is **the** corporation itself.

When selling a corporation — for whatever reason — three different sets of tax laws apply. There is the tax effect on the shareholders (Sec. 331). There is the tax effect on the corporation which is sold (Sec. 336). There is a tax effect on the acquiring corporation (Sec. 338). We will touch on each of these effects.

First, the effect on shareholders. The basic tax law on point is IRC Section 331. The full title of this section is: *Gain or Loss to Shareholders in Corporate Liquidations*. Its subsection (a) is titled: *Distributions in Complete Liquidation Treated as Exchanges*. This subsection reads in full as—

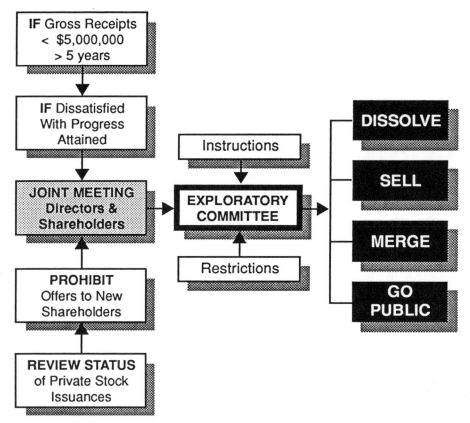

Fig. 12.1 - A Close Corporations Analysis When Growth Goals Not Achieved

*Amounts received by a shareholder in a distribution in **complete liquidation** of a corporation shall be treated as in full payment in exchange for the stock.* [Emphasis added.]

Note the emphasized term: *complete liquidation.* The word "complete" means winding down all of the affairs of the corporation, and doing so within a 12-month period. This includes the distribution of all retained earnings, whether appropriated or unappropriated. The winding down must be preceded by a Plan of Liquidation that is set in motion by a formal resolution by the directors of the corporation. No exchange of the shareholders' stock takes place until the company ceases operations. The last act of "closing the books" on the corporation is to cancel all shares outstanding and pay proceeds pro rata to each shareholder.

The payment of the closing out residuals to shareholders is called: *liquidating distributions.* Said distributions may be cash or noncash (at fair market value). Whatever the final form of payment, the shareholders treat their distributions as gain or loss on the sale of capital assets: NOT as ordinary dividends. Each shareholder's basis for determining the amount of capital gain or capital loss was that which we discussed in Chapter 11: Basis in Stock Held.

All liquidating distributions to shareholders are reported by the corporation to the IRS via Form 1099-DIV. The information is entered on each shareholder's Schedule D (Form 1040): *Capital Gains and Losses.* The general sequence that takes place for shareholders is depicted in Figure 12.2. The end effect is that all stock in the corporation is sold/exchanged in one bulk transaction.

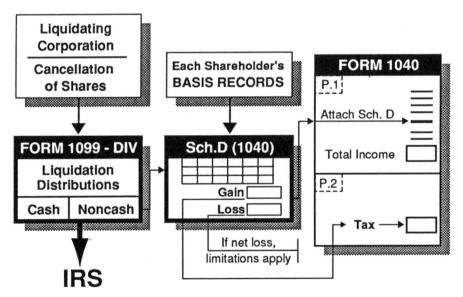

Fig. 12.2 - Sequence of Events When a Corporation Is Liquidated

Effect of Sale on Corporation

The corporation itself experiences a tax effect when it is sold in a bulk transaction. It makes no difference whether a C or S corporation is involved. The corporation is treated as having sold its assets independently of the exchange of shareholders' stock. It is as though two separate transactions took place: I, sale of assets of the corporation and finalizing its own tax return accounting, and II, the exchange of the residual net worth (after corporate taxes) for cancellation of all stock. Such is the mandate of IRC Section 336.

Section 336 is titled: *Gain or Loss Recognized on Property Distributed in Complete Liquidation.* Here, the term "property" means money (cash) and marketable items in lieu of money (noncash). Subsection (a), the general rule therewith, reads—

> *Except as otherwise provided in this section . . . gain or loss shall be recognized to a liquidating corporation on the distribution of property in complete liquidation as if such property were sold to the distributee at its fair market value.* [Emphasis added.]

Note that, again, the term "complete liquidation" appears. This means that a Resolution and Plan of Liquidation must be adopted at a joint meeting of shareholders and directors. The plan must indicate the date on which the meeting was held, the number of voting shares present (including proxies), the date of sale and name of the buyer, the date the liquidation is to be completed, and the number of shares which adopted the resolution. The resolution and its adoption should be authenticated by two officers of the corporation, whose signatures are certified by a Notary Public. One certified copy is sent to the Secretary of State where the corporation was incorporated. When the liquidation is complete, a Final Resolution is adopted and forwarded to the same Secretary of State, for official recording.

For federal purposes, Form 966: *Corporate Dissolution or Liquidation* needs to be prepared. This form is filed with the IRS within 30 days after the Plan of Liquidation is adopted. If the plan is amended before the liquidation is complete, an amended Form 966 is required. The Form 966 and its amendments (if any) also are required to be attached to the final tax return for the corporation (Form 1120 or Form 1120S). There is a checkbox on each return for indicating: ☐ *Final return.*

The "except as otherwise" reference in subsection 336(a) relates to: (b) treatment of liabilities, (c) liquidations which are part of a reorganization, (d) limitations on recognition of loss, (e) certain stock sales treated as asset transfers, and (Sec. 337) property distributed to parent in liquidation of its subsidiary. The idea is for the corporation to clean up all of its tax accounting affairs, including the accommodation of its creditors, before making final distribution to shareholders. The position that we have taken is that your corporation is not a parent of other subsidiaries, nor are you a subsidiary of a parent corporation.

Treatment as "Sale of Assets"

There are situations where a purchasing corporation wants to buy a smaller corporation in its entirety: stock, assets, and all. If it requires 80% or more of the outstanding stock of a selling corporation within 12 months' time, IRC Section 338 applies. This section enables the purchasing corporation to *elect* to treat the stock purchase as asset acquisitions. This election is particularly important where the selling corporation has privately-held stock which has no readily ascertainable market value of its own. In such a case, the purchase price is based on the grossed-up value of the selling corporation's assets: not its stock.

Section 338 is titled: *Certain Stock Purchases Treated as Asset Acquisitions*. Section 338 was first enacted in 1982, and has been amended several times since then. The amendments were for coordination with Section 1060: *Special Allocation Rules for Certain Asset Acquisitions*, which was enacted in 1986 for noncorporate purchasers of a small business. Section 338 comprises about 2,500 words of tax law which are supported by about 80,000 words of regulations. Section 1060 comprises about 750 tax law words supported by about 10,000 words of regulations. There is no way that we can adequately familiarize you with all details of these two IR Code sections. The best we can do is to focus on the intent of what these two sections seek to accomplish.

For years prior to 1986, sellers and buyers of businesses worked the tax laws to each party's advantage. Take goodwill and going concern value, for example. A seller chose to maximize the value of goodwill so as to derive capital gain benefit. This enabled the seller to minimize the *recapture* of his tax attributes (depreciation/depletion allowances, operating loss offsets, capital loss carryovers, unappropriated retained earnings, etc.). Conversely, a buyer chose to minimize the seller's goodwill because it was to be treated as a capital asset, frozen on the buyer's books. By minimizing goodwill, a buyer could maximize the value of depreciable, depletable, amortizable, and expensible assets for better subsequent tax benefits. The intent of Sections 338 and 1060 was to mandate that the tax positions of the seller and buyer **be consistent** with each other. What the seller reports, the buyer also reports. And vice versa. The key for doing so is the requirement that all assets of a transaction be allocated into specific classes.

At present, five specific classes are indicated, though proposed regulations seek seven specific classes. Under the proposed seven classes, the selling price of a business must be allocated as follows:

Class I: Cash and cash equivalents;

Class II: Certificates of deposit, readily marketable stock, securities, or foreign currency;

Class III: Accounts receivable, mortgages, and credit card receivables;

Class IV: Property included in inventory held primarily for sale to customers;

Class V: All assets not in Classes I, II, III, VI, or VII

Class VI: All Code Sec. 197 intangibles, except those in the nature of goodwill and going concern value, and:

Class VII: Goodwill and going concern value.
[Note: Sec. 197 is titled: *Amortization of Goodwill and Certain Other Intangibles.*]

For complying with Sections 338 and 1060, the following two IRS forms are required:

Form 8023: *Elections under Section 338 for Corporations Making Qualified Stock Purchases*, and
Form 8594: *Asset Acquisition Statement under Section 1060.*

Both forms are filed with the tax return for each entity for the year of acquisition of the corporation sold. Both entities must agree to the information and values entered. As arduous as these forms may be, they markedly reduce controversies with the IRS concerning gain, loss, and recapture computations by the selling entity, and new basis starts by the acquiring entity.

Stock-for-Stock Exchanges

Selling a privately-held small business corporation is not always satisfying to the wealth building aspirations of the controlling shareholders. In some cases, it is better to merge with a larger corporation and take up an ownership position in the merged entity. This effort is particularly attractive if the acquiring corporation holds publicly-traded stock. The goal would be the exchange of private stock for public stock using the grossed-up asset value of the target corporation as the equity basis for the exchange.

The merger approach ventures into the exciting world of mergers and acquisitions called: *reorganizations*. The excitement stems from IRC Section 354: *Exchanges of Stock and Securities in Certain Reorganizations*. Section 354 is the genesis of **tax-free** rules for certain statutorily prescribed reorganizations. This is the significance of the statutory phrase: "No gain or loss . . ." etc. The tax-free exchange concept goes way back to 1954. Its amendments have been refinements rather than substantive changes in the concept of exchanges.

The essence of Section 354 is its subsection (a): General Rule. Its paragraph (1) reads in full—

*No gain or loss shall be recognized if **stock or securities** in a corporation a party to a reorganization are, in pursuance of a plan of reorganization, **exchanged solely for** stock or securities in such corporation or in another corporation a party to the reorganization.* [Emphasis added.]

The key to tax-free exchange success is an understanding of the terms: "stock or securities," "exchanged solely for," under "a plan of reorganization." Otherwise, the *Limitations* of paragraph (2) of subsection (a) come into focus. Paragraph (2) stresses that paragraph (1) does not apply to those cases where there is:

(A) Excess principal amount,
(B) Property attributable to accrued interest,
(C) Nonqualified preferred stock, and
(D) Recapitalization of family-owned corporations.

While these items do not participate in the tax-free process, they do not disqualify those items which can be clearly identified as: "stock or securities." The courts have consistently taken the position that the term "or" has the same meaning as "and": stock *and* securities. In reality, not one or the other is solely exchanged; a combination of both stock and securities is exchanged.

The term "stock" is generally understood to mean common stock only. This is the pure risk portion of corporate ownership. Preferred stock, bonds, debentures, notes, stock rights, dividend rights, etc. are broadly classed as "securities." They are so classed because they are characterized by a continuity of interest in the affairs and future earnings of a corporation.

There is a trick to achieving success in a tax-free reorganization exchange. It is a meeting of minds re the identification of assets, methods of valuation and accounting, and a matching of the bulk valuation of the target corporation's stock and securities with the acquiring corporation's offer of its stock and securities. As we depict in Figure 12.3, the exchange principle is simple. It is the clash of egos and the pounding of desks that can make the process difficult and disagreeable.

Types of Reorganizations

To qualify as a tax-free reorganization, the reorganization must fall within one of seven categories described by Section 368(a). This section is titled: ***Definitions Relating to Corporate Reorganizations***. This section comprises approximately 2,750 statutory words. We'd rather paraphrase the essence of the seven types of reorganizations that are described. There about 2,000 words of special rules that apply, which we will not get into.

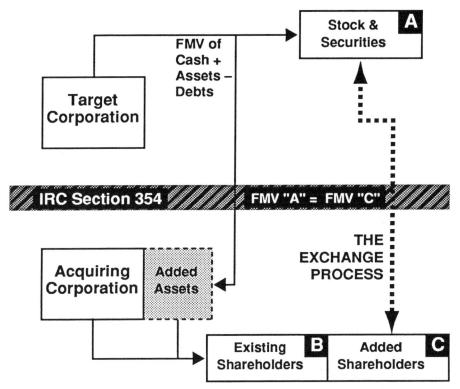

Fig. 12.3 - Exchange of Stock in Tax-Free Corporate Reorganizations

Accordingly, the qualifying types of reorganizations are:

1. Type "A" Reorganization
   — statutory merger or consolidation;
2. Type "B" Reorganization
   — exchanges of controlling stock for voting stock in an acquiring corporation;
3. Type "C" Reorganization
   — exchanges of substantially all assets for voting stock in an acquiring corporation;
4. Type "D" Reorganization
   — transfers of all or a part of assets to a corporation in which the transferring shareholders control the acquiring corporation;

5. Type "E" Reorganization
   — reshuffling of a corporation's capital structure with no virtual change in control;
6. Type "F" Reorganization
   — a mere change in identity, form, or place of organization; and
7. Type "G" Reorganization
   — a bankruptcy transfer of assets pursuant to a court-approved reorganization plan.

In all of these reorganization types, there are three common statutory requirements. These requirements are: (1) control, (2) substantially all assets, and (3) continuity of business. The term "control" means—

The ownership of stock possessing at least 80% of the total combined voting power of all classes of stock entitled to vote and at least 80% of the total number of shares of all other classes of stock of the corporation [subsec. 368(c)].

The term "substantially all assets" means the transference from the target corporation to the acquiring corporation of all but a small, necessary, portion of cash and property to pay off reluctant creditors and opposing shareholders of the target corporation. A certain amount of retained assets also is necessary to formally liquidate the target corporation.

The term "continuity of business" means that the acquiring corporation does one of two things with the assets of the target corporation. The acquirer continues the target corporation's most recent line of business. Or, the acquirer uses a significant portion of the target corporation's assets in an enhanced line of business.

The Merger Process Exemplified

A Type "A" reorganization is often preferred among small corporations which want to merge or consolidate and grow big. A consolidation is the combination of two or more corporations forming into a new one, after which the former corporations are dissolved. A merger is similar except that, instead of a new corporation being formed, one of the predecessors retains its identity and continues its existence . . . in strengthened form. The concept of continuance is predicated upon a bona fide business purpose for the reorganization, and the discontinuance or dissolution of the acquired corporation(s).

There is no restriction on the kind of consideration that may be received by the stockholders of the acquired corporation(s). The consideration may be money, property, or other equivalents. So long as the stock and securities that they relinquish are market-equivalent to those that they receive, there is a bona fide tax-free exchange. However, if there is any "boot" (excess over fair market value) received, or if interest accrues because of delays in the exchange accounting and issuance of new shares, the recognition of income is required. This is called: *Receipt of Additional Consideration*, which is taxable pursuant to Section 356.

To illustrate the tax-free effect of consolidating two corporations into a new one, consider Corporation X and Corporation Y. They transfer all of their assets solely for voting stock in a newly formed corporation, the XY Corporation. Corporation X and Corporation Y then transfer the XY stock to their respective shareholders in exchange for the X stock or the Y stock, as the case may be. The X and Y corporations are liquidated, and the two businesses are thereafter carried on by the XY Corporation as one business.

A merger would be similar, except that, instead of the XY Corporation being formed, the Y Corporation, for example, continues its existence. Thereupon, Y stock is exchanged for the X stock held by the X Corporation shareholders. The result, often, is a new combination of controlling interests.

The above arrangement is both an "A" reorganization and a "C" reorganization. It is an "A" type because two formerly unrelated corporations merged. It is also a "C" type because assets were exchanged solely for voting stock.

In a "B" type reorganization, the acquiring corporation simply acquires the controlling stock of the target corporation, by exchanging its voting stock for that of the target's. Immediately after the exchange, the acquiring corporation is in control of the target. Over a period of time thereafter, the merging and consolidating processes are "worked out."

Precautions When "Going Public"

The merging of two or more corporations can result in a clash of business cultures and management egos. The former executives and their staffs jockey for positions of control in the consolidated entity. Before long, one group spins off and seeks to go public on its own. Or, as is more often the case, the preliminary merger negotiations break down. In such event, the more aspiring group for growth and control turns its attention to going public. This process is costly and time consuming; several precautionary steps are required.

The first precaution is at least a modicum of independent familiarity with the Securities Act of 1933, and its zillions of rules and regulations since that time. Scholarly business and law books are available for this purpose. The idea is not to become overwhelmed by the regulatory and procedural enormity of the task. It is to add a touch of humility to an otherwise aggressive and blindsided ego.

The second precaution is to become familiar with Regulation D of the federal Securities and Exchange Commission (SEC). This regulation sets out certain safe harbor exemptions from the public registration of stock and securities, defines accredited (individual net worth over $1 million) and nonaccredited investors, and limits the number of private placements to no more than 35 shareholders. Private offerings up to $7.5 million worth of securities require specific disclosure statements to the SEC, as well as to state securities agencies. It is always prudent to review and comply with all disclosure requirements re the private shares already issued. We warned you earlier about tripping into a public offering mode.

The third precaution is to familiarize yourself with SEC Form S-1: *Registration Statement under the Securities Act of 1933*. If you can, get a blank copy of this form and its instructions. Review it with the idea of absorbing the scope and depth of information necessary for its completion. Particularly note the rules on calculating the Registration Fee, who must sign the statement as the

Registrant, and which principal officers and directors must sign. Do not contact a securities law firm at this point, as you want to know on your own what will be expected of you and your corporation. Law firms want big money up front . . . before educating you on the pitfalls you face.

The fourth familiarization precaution is to get a copy of the 50 pages or so of general instructions for an *Offering Statement under Regulation A*. The contents of this statement are summarized and (very) highly abbreviated in Figure 12.4.

OFFERING STATEMENT UNDER SEC REGULATION A	
Item	**Matters Covered**
1 The Company	Name, date of incorporation, principal office
2 Risk Factors	List & discuss in order of importance
3 Products & Services	Nature of business & order backlog
4 Offering Price	Projected price/earnings multiples
5 Use of Proceeds	Salaries, debt retirement, new assets, etc.
6 Capitalization	Anticipation of liquidity & cash flow
7 Description of Stock	Common, preferred, voting rights, limitations
8 Plan of Distribution	Issuance goal, selling agents, commissions
9 Dividends & Redemptions	History of, within last 5 years
10 Officers of the Company	Name, age, education, experience, conflicts
11 Directors of the Company	Name, age, experience, hours devoted
12 Principal Stockholders	Those holding 10% before initial offering
13 Executive Pay	List total compensation: cash, stock, other
14 Litigation Prospects	Describe past, present, or threatened
15 Federal Tax Aspects	Potential benefits & possible disallowances
16 Miscellaneous Factors	Either favorable or adverse to operations
17 Financial Statements	Profit & loss, pro forma, balance sheets
18 Analysis by Management	Past results, future prospects, gross margins

Fig. 12.4 - Items of Disclosure When Offering Stock to Public

As to describing the risk factors (item 2 in Figure 12.4), the official instructions say—

The Company should avoid generalized statements and include only those factors which are unique to the Company. No specific number of risk factors is required to be identified. . . . Risk may be due to such matters as cash flow and liquidity problems, inexperience of management, dependence of the Company on an unproven product, absence of an existing market for the product (even though management may believe a need exists), the nature of the business in which the Company is engaged or proposes to engage, conflicts of interest with management, arbitrary establishment of offering price, absence of a trading market if a trading market is not expected to develop . . . etc.

By the time you have digested a good portion of the above, you are ready to begin making inquiries to securities underwriters and securities law firms. You will not be able to launch a public offering without their services. Securities underwriting and legal representation do not come cheap. Get estimates of their costs and shop around. Do not be surprised if the cost approaches $1 million.

Tax Law Statement

Item 15 in Figure 12.4 requires a discourse on those federal taxation matters that may affect new investors. The SEC instruction in this regard says, in part—

If . . . it is anticipated that any significant tax benefits will be available to investors in this offering, indicate the nature and amount of such anticipated tax benefits and the material risks of their disallowance.

This SEC instruction is a golden opportunity to acquaint new investors with Internal Revenue Code Section 1202: *50 Percent Exclusion for Gain from Certain Small Business Stock.* Its general rule, subsection (a) reads in full as—

In the case of a taxpayer other than a corporation, gross income shall not include 50 percent of any gain from the sale or exchange of qualified small business stock held for more than 5 years.

The bottom line essence of Section 1202(a) is that, if the corporation grows in five years as anticipated, a new investor will pay only 10% in federal tax on his capital gains [50% x 20% (subsec. 1(h)(1)(C)]. This is the consequence of new tax law enacted on August 10, 1993. It is not securities marketing hype.

Congress enacted Section 1202 with the express intention of encouraging public investment in new ventures and small businesses. To receive the 10% tax rate benefits, the stock must be issued by a *qualified small business*. As per subsection (d), such a business is defined as—

Any domestic corporation which is a C corporation [whose] aggregate gross assets . . . before . . . and immediately after the issuance (determined by taking into account amounts received in the issuance) do not exceed $50,000,000 [50 million].

There is also an *active business requirement*, subsection (e), which requires that the corporation devote—

At least 80 percent (by value) of the assets . . . in the active conduct of 1 or more qualified trades or businesses . . . [which are] other than—

(A)   performance of professional services (health, engineering, law, etc.),
(B)   banking, insurance, financial, etc.
(C)   farming, fishing, ranching, etc.
(D)   extraction or production of natural resources, and
(E)   operating a hotel, motel, restaurant, etc.

Issuance Goal: 10 Times Assets

In the registration statement for its initial public offering (IPO), the corporation is to indicate its target goal of the issuance. The maximum/minimum price per share is to be established, as well as the maximum/minimum target proceeds. It is the NET PROCEEDS (total proceeds less offering expenses) of the IPO that accrues to the corporation's gross assets. Accordingly, a respectable target goal would be at least 10 times the current (before IPO) gross assets of the company.

For example, assume that your corporation's current gross assets (cash plus adjusted basis of all property except stock) are $5,000,000 (5 million). As per above, the target goal of issuance would be $50,000,000 (50 million). When this point is reached, any stock issued beyond $50 million would not qualify for the 50% exclusion of capital gain under Section 1202(a). Your corporation's underwriting agent would have to inform the excess subscribers (if any) of this fact.

Throughout this book, our premise has been that the corporation of which you are a shareholder is classed as "small" by industry standards. For this classification, three common yardsticks are used. These are: (1) gross assets, (2) gross receipts (for the most current taxable year), and (3) gross value of all (privately placed) stock outstanding. In *general*, if each of these yardsticks is at or below $5,000,000 ($5 million), the corporation is considered small. This is the size range for which the "testing" (development and marketing) of a new product idea is near-ideal.

To go beyond the $5 million range, merging with an existing public corporation or going public on your own is the more practical arena for significant growth. Before going public, however, you have to disclose to the world **all** of your private corporation's tax, accounting, financial, management, and executive pay problems of the past. If you do this honestly and prudently, you should be able to avoid the distress of most post-IPO setbacks.

The public stock arena is certainly where opportunities for enhanced personal wealth of the original founders and principals of the small corporation lie. The push to go public should not be premature. Make sure that your product, service, or great idea has been adequately tested. Then, in your initial offering prospectus, set the tone of your growth and profit projections in modest and realistic terms.

ABOUT

THE AUTHOR

Holmes F. Crouch

Born on a small farm in southern Maryland, Holmes was graduated from the U.S. Coast Guard Academy with a Bachelor's Degree in Marine Engineering. While serving on active duty, he wrote many technical articles on maritime matters. After attaining the rank of Lieutenant Commander, he resigned to pursue a career as a nuclear engineer.

Continuing his education, he earned a Master's Degree in Nuclear Engineering from the University of California. He also authored two books on nuclear propulsion. As a result of the tax write-offs associated with writing these books, the IRS audited his returns. The IRS's handling of the audit procedure so annoyed Holmes that he undertook to become as knowledgeable as possible regarding tax procedures. He became a licensed private Tax Practitioner by passing an examination administered by the IRS. Having attained this credential, he started his own tax preparation and counseling business in 1972.

In the early years of his tax practice, he was a regular talk-show guest on San Francisco's KGO Radio responding to hundreds of phone-in tax questions from listeners. He was a much sought-after guest speaker at many business seminars and taxpayer meetings. He also provided counseling on special tax problems, such as divorce matters, property exchanges, timber harvesting, mining ventures, animal breeding, independent contractors, selling businesses, and offices-at-home. Over the past 25 years, he has prepared nearly 10,000 tax returns for individuals, estates, trusts, and small businesses (in partnership and corporate form).

During the tax season of January through April, he prepares returns in a unique manner. During a single meeting, he completes the return . . . *on the spot!* The client leaves with his return signed, sealed, and in a stamped envelope. His unique approach to preparing returns and his personal interest in his clients' tax affairs have honed his professional proficiency. His expertise extends through itemized deductions, computer-matching of income sources, capital gains and losses, business expenses and cost of goods, residential rental expenses, limited and general partnership activities, closely-held corporations, to family farms and ranches.

He remembers spending 12 straight hours completing a doctor's complex return. The next year, the doctor, having moved away, utilized a large accounting firm to prepare his return. Their accountant was so impressed by the manner in which the prior return was prepared that he recommended the doctor travel the 500 miles each year to have Holmes continue doing it.

He recalls preparing a return for an unemployed welder, for which he charged no fee. Two years later the welder came back and had his return prepared. He paid the regular fee . . . and then added a $300 tip.

During the off season, he represents clients at IRS audits and appeals. In one case a shoe salesman's audit was scheduled to last three hours. However, after examining Holmes' documentation it was concluded in 15 minutes with "no change" to his return. In another instance he went to an audit of a custom jeweler that the IRS dragged out for more than six hours. But, supported by Holmes' documentation, the client's return was accepted by the IRS with "no change."

Then there was the audit of a language translator that lasted two full days. The auditor scrutinized more than $1.25 million in gross receipts, all direct costs, and operating expenses. Even though all expensed items were documented and verified, the auditor decided that more than $23,000 of expenses ought to be listed as capital items for depreciation instead. If this had been enforced it would have resulted in a significant additional amount of tax. Holmes strongly disagreed and after many hours of explanation got the amount reduced by more than 60% on behalf of his client.

He has dealt extensively with gift, death and trust tax returns. These preparations have involved him in the tax aspects of wills, estate planning, trustee duties, probate, marital and charitable bequests, gift and death exemptions, and property titling.

Although not an attorney, he prepares Petitions to the U.S. Tax Court for clients. He details the IRS errors and taxpayer facts by citing pertinent sections of tax law and regulations. In a recent case involving an attorney's ex-spouse, the IRS asserted a tax deficiency of $155,000. On behalf of his client, he petitioned the Tax Court and within six months the IRS conceded the case.

Over the years, Holmes has observed that the IRS is not the industrious, impartial, and competent federal agency that its official public imaging would have us believe.

He found that, at times, under the slightest pretext, the IRS has interpreted against a taxpayer in order to assess maximum penalties, and may even delay pending matters so as to increase interest due on additional taxes. He has confronted the IRS in his own behalf on five separate occasions, going before the U.S. Claims Court, U.S. District Court, and U.S. Tax Court. These were court actions that tested specific sections of the Internal Revenue Code which he found ambiguous, inequitable, and abusively interpreted by the IRS.

Disturbed by the conduct of the IRS and by the general lack of tax knowledge by most individuals, he began an innovative series of taxpayer-oriented Federal tax guides. To fulfill this need, he undertook the writing of a series of guidebooks that provide in-depth knowledge on one tax subject at a time. He focuses on subjects that plague taxpayers all throughout the year. Hence, his formulation of the "Allyear" Tax Guide series.

The author is indebted to his wife, Irma Jean, and daughter, Barbara MacRae, for the word processing and computer graphics that turn his experiences into the reality of these publications. Holmes welcomes comments, questions, and suggestions from his readers. He can be contacted in California at (408) 867-2628, or by writing to the publisher's address.

ALLYEAR Tax Guides
by Holmes F. Crouch

Series 100 - INDIVIDUALS AND FAMILIES

BEING SELF-EMPLOYED .... T/G 101
DEDUCTING JOB EXPENSES .... T/G 102
FAMILY TAX STRATEGIES .... T/G 103
RESOLVING DIVORCE ISSUES .... T/G 104
CITIZENS WORKING ABROAD .... T/G 105

Series 200 - INVESTORS AND BUSINESSES

INVESTOR GAINS & LOSSES .... T/G 201
PROFITS, TAXES, & LLCs...................................... T/G 202
STARTING YOUR BUSINESS .... T/G 203
MAKING PARTNERSHIPS WORK .... T/G 204
SMALL C & S CORPORATIONS.............................. T/G 205

Series 300 - RETIREES AND ESTATES

DECISIONS WHEN RETIRING .... T/G 301
WRITING YOUR WILL .... T/G 302
SIMPLIFYING YOUR ESTATE .... T/G 303
YOUR EXECUTOR DUTIES .... T/G 304
YOUR TRUSTEE DUTIES .... T/G 305

Series 400 - OWNERS AND SELLERS

RENTAL REAL ESTATE .... T/G 401
OWNING NATURAL RESOURCES .... T/G 402
FAMILY TRUSTS & TRUSTORS............................... T/G 403
SELLING YOUR HOME(S)....................................... T/G 404
SELLING YOUR BUSINESS .... T/G 405

Series 500 - AUDITS AND APPEALS

KEEPING GOOD RECORDS .... T/G 501
WINNING YOUR AUDIT... T/G 502
DISAGREEING WITH THE IRS .... T/G 503
CONTESTING IRS PENALTIES .... T/G 504
GOING INTO TAX COURT .... T/G 505

For information about the above titles,
and/or a free 8 page catalog, contact:

www.allyeartax.com

Phone: (408) 867-2628   Fax: (408) 867-6466